# NEED-TO-KNOW
# MARKETING

# NEED-TO-KNOW MARKETING

## AN ACCESSIBLE
## A to Z
### GUIDE

# Tim Ambler

C

CENTURY
**BUSINESS**

First published in 1992 in Great Britain by
Century Business
An imprint of Random House UK Limited
20 Vauxhall Bridge Road, London SW1V 2SA

Random House Australia (Pty) Limited
20 Alfred Street, Milsons Point, Sydney
New South Wales 2061, Australia

Random House New Zealand Limited
18 Poland Road, Glenfield
Auckland 10, New Zealand

Random House South Africa (Pty) Limited
PO Box 337, Bergvlei, South Africa

Set in Baskerville by Edna A. Moore
𝞣 Tek-Art, Addiscombe, Croydon, Surrey

Printed and bound in Great Britain by
Mackays of Chatham PLC, Chatham, Kent

British Library Cataloguing in Publication Data
A catalogue record for this book is available from the British Library

ISBN 0-7126-9834-5

Companies, institutions and other organizations wishing to make bulk
purchases of this title or any other Century Business publication
should contact:

Direct Sales Manager
Century Business
Random House
20 Vauxhall Bridge Road
London SW1V 2SA
Fax: 071-828 6681

# Contents

# Acknowledgements

This book is a collection of some things old, some new, some borrowed. The publishers mostly censored the blue. I am most grateful to all who, knowingly or not, have contributed to the development of these personal views. Many kind people in International Distillers and Vintners, the wine and spirit trade, Grand Metropolitan and, more recently, London Business School have tolerated ignorant questions and decisions and then taught me all I know about marketing. Some sources are listed below and some at the end of the chapter on Kotler.

At the same time I must stress that none of these views are necessarily shared by them or other colleagues old or new. These are not the opinions of GrandMet nor London Business School. Some are well rooted in facts and research; some are just quizzical reflections arising from half a life time in marketing around the world. Inaccuracies, errors and omissions are entirely my responsibility. Please write to point them out. Writing a book turned out to be an education in what I did not know. Examples or counter-examples which challenge the assertions here would be especially welcome.

Particular appreciation is due to those friends and colleagues who have read drafts, provided comments and encouraged this book to happen.

I am most grateful to George Bull, Paul Curtis, Clive Holland, Arthur Hopkins, Don Knight, Peter Lane, Rod Scarth and Peter Thompson (Training and I.S.) and Brian Sands and Lance Wilson (Information Systems) for reading and commenting. Also, at London Business School, Paddy Barwise, Laura Cousins and Jens Maier (Planning), John Cripps, Tom Robertson and Kathryn Vagneur.

The production team did a marvellous job despite the vagaries of the author. Many thanks to Elizabeth Hennessy and her colleagues at Random House, to Spider Jenkins and Jenny Stratton who coped with manuscript amendments and especially to Morgan Witzel who translated much of the text into English.

I want to thank Grand Metropolitan also for their generous support of my Fellowship at London Business School.

Finally, and most of all, to Kate to whom this book is dedicated in the hope that the threats made whilst it was in gestation will not be implemented.

To all those, and many more, I really am most grateful.

*Dear Val,*                              *Friday Lunchtime*

Congratulations on your appointment as SBU CEO. Does this make you a person of letters? Chief Executive of such a major business at your age is impressive indeed. I was delighted to hear that you wanted to take a fresh look at marketing. Any business depends for its now and future livelihood on its brands and products, customers and the end consumers. Profit is created by bringing these elements into positive relationships. That is marketing.

Can you be up to speed by Monday? In this wonderful world where reality is image and tangible products are but a bundle of perceptions, marketing people pass through the looking glass several times a day. The weekend gives us plenty of time.

You want stunning marketing. That requires the right environment for marketing talent to flourish. This book reviews the fundamental marketing mix, the four Ps of Product, Price, Promotion and Place, competitive issues, management and organizational development. There are some flights of philosophy but the focus is ruthlessly pragmatic. Each chapter is spiced with variety as befits the weekend but is serious too: we are talking serious money. There is a bias to branded consumer goods, and the drinks business within that, since that is my background. I know you are well able to translate those lessons into your own business. Every chapter ends with action points expressed as a memo to file.

Marketing is not for those who expect neat and tidy answers. Here the conventional mixes with the eccentric. Challenges and novelties rub paragraphs with traditional beliefs. The book is a bran tub. Dip in anywhere and question what you bring out. See the book as a marketplace of its own: chapters and ideas compete with one another for your attention. Are they consistent? Why should they be?

Marketing textbooks draw heavily on the micro-economists' models of the world. Analysis, logic and order are certainly important but do not put wealth in the wallet. Success needs imagination, intuition and even manic determination. Trying to impose neat order on an untidy market is madder than enjoying the insanity of it all. If you really must meet marketing in a logical order, a route map has, reluctantly, been provided as Appendix 2.

This is a lateral book. The challenges and assertions are there to spark just a few live connections. Even one can be enough to release the spirit of innovation that triggers successful marketing. Conventional wisdom belongs to the competition. The more **they** research, the more **they** analyse, the more **you** have to be different.

Enjoy the weekend. This is a book to relax to. Filter it through that mental twilight where the impossible becomes likely. Suspend disbelief and allow the subconscious to retain only what it needs. You have been under stress; take it easy now. If you have visitors, plead pressure of work. Read this book in the bath or under the apple tree or in the back of your new Bentley.

Good luck in your new job. Release the talents of your new team and remember: the best marketing in the world can only give luck a chance.

*Yours affectionately,*

*Tim*

# A

# 1.   Advertising kite high

**ISSUES:**

1. Why is advertising important to the marketer?
2. What does advertising do?
3. How does the advertising system work?
4. How should decisions be made?

Whenever you book a table at the very latest restaurant, you can be sure your advertising agency was there the week before. Advertising may not belong at the beginning of marketing, but its initial letter gets it ahead. What else do you know that got in before the serpent advertised apples to Eve? Maybe advertising gave serpents a bad name.

## 1.   THE IMPORTANCE OF ADVERTISING

Modern marketing began with advertising. Newspapers and magazines had space to fill; advertising agents sold it. In the 1880s, F W Ayer first recognized the potential of providing advertisers with copy, artwork and media advice and founded the first advertising agency. He called it N W Ayer and Son because he thought his father's image was better. A few years later, he established the 15 per cent commission rate on openly disclosed space charges. This eventually became the standard in both the UK and USA, and has survived generations of alternatives which mostly involve fees from the 'client', i.e. the bill paying advertiser. That the agent is paid by the media, not the advertiser, is still important today. The expression 'above the line' refers to the line drawn between work remunerated by the media and that paid by the client.

The role of advertising agent was to design messages to fit both the consumer's and the product's needs. The agent's independence from the manufacturer allowed him to see products from the consumer's point of view and consumers from the producer's situation. In the 1930s Rosser Reeves, later a co-founder of the Ted Bates agency, first described the importance of the 'Unique Selling Proposition' as a communication bridge between product and consumer. The consumer wanted to know, concisely, what the brand offered him or her; the marketer needed to know where the brand's strength lay. The vocabulary has changed but that concept still sits at the heart of differentiating or positioning a brand.

Just as advertising was a progenitor of consumer brand marketing, so that in turn begat the myriad forms of marketing that exist today: industrial, retail, business to business, network, services, direct, database, internal and on. This chapter concentrates on advertising for fast moving consumer goods ('fmcg') because that tradition throws branding into high relief. Marketing is a broad church and includes those who doubt the centrality of branding. No such doubts exist here: marketing is the business of adding value for consumers, customers and marketers alike. The brand is the entity that carries that added value and the essence of all forms of marketing.

Today, advertising and marketing are frequently confused. To the general public, advertising is the most conspicuous sign of marketing. In the 1950s and 60s many companies had their marketing function handled by their advertising agency. Some still do. But since the last century, the scales have progressively tipped to the point where advertising has become just one element in the communications sector of a marketing programme alongside public relations, promotions, direct methods using electronic databases, and personal selling.

Confusion between advertising and marketing is not limited to the general public. Effective communication requires the marketer to simplify the brand proposition and select perhaps only one of its many appeals. To reinforce the advertising, other marketing activities will be similarly focused.

Television created the golden age of advertising. This friendly intruder into almost every home achieved more attention to fewer channels than any medium in history. Television was the vehicle to persuade the mass millions. Through the 1950s and into the 1970s, fmcg brand owners rushed to exploit television's potential.

New technology brought alternative channels: cable, satellites, video, Walkmans and CDs. Print media choice multiplied. With the growing strength of retailers, budgets were diverted to 'promotions', a word that has gradually shifted its meaning to embrace many different marketing activities. Often it is simply a cloak for discount to the retailers. The economic troughs of 1974, 1981 and 1990 added to the pressure on the advertiser to cut fat and the agency to provide the fat to be cut.

Some advertisers claim that the changes have been refreshing: agencies have to be more attentive to client demands, and to stick more closely to their three key functions of creative content, media buying and client service. Fewer people in client marketing departments will not increase the agencies' service costs, but will reduce the service demanded (or so clients claim). However, not all advertising executives are persuaded. With business hard to get and/or keep, few agencies will criticize their clients in public, although in private and sometimes in the trade media, they are increasingly concerned with arbitrary behaviour, decision-making and interference by clients which can lead to lower advertising quality.

Contentious it may be but the relative size of a marketing budget and advertising within that is a measure, not the best but still significant, of brand strength. It has a certain macho appeal. I spend, therefore I am, could be a tenet of brand management, even if it does put Descartes before the stable door. That a brand needs and is sustained by a large media budget is likely to indicate that it is an important brand. The reverse is not true: many valuable brands in industrial markets have minimal advertising expenditure. Of course, the real value of a brand has more to do with profitability, price premium and volume but the symbolic impact of advertising should not be overlooked.

## 2.  WHAT ADVERTISING DOES

There are many models of consumer responses to advertising, but most deal with consumer awareness and consumer attitudes. These attitudes may refer to brand use, perceptions of quality and other users, packaging, style, heritage. The probability of purchase is heightened by positive associations of the brand name. These associations, positive and negative, are supposed to flit through the consumer's mind as he or she makes a choice. But before advertising can go to work to improve these attitudes, the consumer has to know about, or be aware of, the brand.

The classic measure of awareness is obtained by asking respondents which brands came into their heads when a category was mentioned (this is known as 'top of mind' or 'unaided recall') and then prompting them with a list of the brands of interest. Adding the two percentages together gives 'total awareness', however illogical that may sound. Modern research breaks awareness down further to many different dimensions depending on the associations being used as prompts. We do not need to worry about these here.

Attitudes are measured by consumer reactions to a battery of questions with answers usually on a five point scale. An example might be, 'indicate on the scale from *agree very much* to *totally disagree* your response to the statement: Nike is the best shoe for top runners.'

Awareness and attitudes measures of the effectiveness of advertising will, however, be muddied by experience of usage and word of mouth from friends and acquaintances. These can be more powerful than advertising which is a weak force with the consumer, and probably getting weaker.

Breaking through the clutter of competing messages with such a weak force is quite a problem. Visibility is not just the adrenalin of advertising, it is also the rationale behind it. This is show business. Many believe that in advertising one should spend big or spend nothing; dribbling it out wastes money. But there are always counter examples to any such convention. In the Scotch whisky market, first Bells and then Famous Grouse built credibility through years of small displays which faded into the wall paper. A plumber just needs to hang out his sign where the householder with a problem will find it. Nevertheless, the convention that fmcg brands should consolidate their advertising into solid punchy blocks has had some academic support.

Within our fmcg convention, consumer response, i.e. sales volume, follows an S shaped curve. This is not the only model but it is a useful one. The cost of advertising has been shown as a straight line in the idealized diagram below. Although discounts are available for higher spending, they may be offset by the need to use less efficient media as the budget increases.

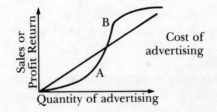

*Figure 1    Consumer response to advertising*

At the beginning of the curve, impressions are swamped by everything else in the media. Impact is limited. Spend more over time and there may be a breakthrough, shown as A on the diagram. Once the awareness impact begins, attitudes may begin to move and advertising becomes cost-efficient. At point A, it is beginning to achieve response at a greater rate than it is costing. Suddenly there is impact for the advertising (and, if the client is lucky, for his brand).

The first turning point is not easy to find, nor is the second.

B marks the stage where advertising starts to have declining returns. In theory, therefore, one should bunch one's spending into peaks to target the consumer response peaks. In this model, spending all the budget to achieve point B maximizes both awareness and the positive benefit to brand attitudes. All one has to do is find the money and find the B spot! Where the budget is justified, spending should be concentrated into separate pulses each of which is targeted to hit B, with an intermission before the next pulse.

The consumer response function explains why advertisers will take space at famous events even though the costs per thousand are disproportionately expensive. A showcase setting should bring more attention, perhaps even glamour.

The US Super Bowl is a classic example of an advertising 'high': a burst of creativity, a burst of expenditure and, hopefully, a widening circle of increased brand awareness and improved attitudes. That does not make the Super Bowl good value for money. It is priced out of reach of all but the few. Advertising during the 1991 US Super Bowl cost $1,700,000 per minute. One company, Master Lock, spends its total budget, each year, on just one Super Bowl ad. High visibility, high adrenalin and doubtless a few seats and highballs for the top customers.

## 3. WORKING THE ADVERTISING SYSTEM

### Managing relationships

Escalating costs, media proliferation, declining returns and recession have put client-agency relationships under strain. In the UK, the Rover car company rang warning bells by turning its business to one of its own executives who left to set up a new agency. The threat was clear and it was not just the money. If a marketer could do the agency's job, where would it end?

Money is a chunk of the problem; results are another. According to the Media Audits' 1992 survey, 42 per cent of UK advertisers think agencies are defrauding their clients to boost their incomes. The smaller spenders are the more suspicious. 72

per cent would like to pay by results and 12 per cent already do. The overall picture, probably alarmist, is one of confusion and dissent.

Once again the respective roles of advertiser and the agency are under review. How should marketers manage the advertising process?

First, the marketers must recognize that agencies understand advertising better than they do. For one thing, they see a great deal more of it. They also see it off-stage without the tinsel and glitter of the sales pitch. Few clients realize the rejection and elimination that has already taken place before he gets to see the show, especially where the client's judgement commands respect. On the other hand, agencies are in love with advertising and have an excessive idea of their own creativity and what it can achieve. Remuneration is directly geared to the amount of media space the agency persuades the client to accept. Consumers do not have to worry about 'hidden persuaders'; advertisers do.

Those convinced by the positive side of that balance will leave the process largely to the agency. Those worried by the negative side will tend to meddle. It is worth reviewing both points of view.

In the 'hands off' model, marketers select the most appropriate agency, brief their team thoroughly, agree realistic awareness and attitude objectives and leave them to it. Good research (tracking studies) before and after the advertising will assess performance. Fresh objectives, set once a year, indicate areas for improvement; if no improvement occurs, you split. Either way, one might say, the agency is fired with enthusiasm.

In the 'meddling' model, each layer of marketing management insists on approving new concepts before the layer above see them. Every piece of agency arithmetic is double checked and the media buying is double guessed. It is frustrating for creative people to see great ideas killed before the top decision-makers, those most likely to recognize brilliance, ever see them. Safe or derivative advertising or no advertising at all is the likely result. Why should a 25 year old brand manager whose only experience is in merchandizing and promotions judge the work of top advertising professionals?

In fact, both the carrot and the cane have their moments. Every client/agency relationship finds its own pattern. The days when a top agency can discipline its client to accept the house system or leave, as Collett Dickinson Pearce used to do, are gone. Clients are concerned with results more than process. Their first preoccupation is to find the right agency for their brands, and the right agency is not always the best agency even if 'best' could be defined. For instance, small brands tend to sit more comfortably in smaller agencies. And some agencies are more effective in some product categories than others – something few will admit.

Some of the meddling problem will be resolved by staff cutbacks on both sides; the survivors will be too busy to meddle. More than that, top management on both sides need to review performance against objectives and to consider how the relationship can be more productively managed.

## Setting objectives

When top UK marketing practitioners were asked recently what academics could usefully tell them, one of the most popular answers was 'tell us how to work out how much to spend'. For a hundred years knights have been setting out from the Round Table to do that. Over the last 30 they have been doing regression analyses and the like. They have mostly returned sadder and wiser. The Advertising Research Foundation in the US has found light in the tunnel. Dr Lodish, of Wharton, reported some key findings in 1991. In about 50 per cent of 220 tests, the quantity, or weight, of advertising did not appear to affect the responses (sales). Clearly such conclusions need to be examined in detail since at the extremes, weight certainly matters. Their conclusion fits with long held advertising wisdom that quantity is subsidiary to quality. They also concluded that the 'wearout' of advertising took about two years. In the tests they used, sales increased in the first year, year 0, by 22 per cent relative to a control group. In the next two years, the research and control groups had the same advertising weight. The spillover effect was an increase in year 1 of 14 per cent and 7 per cent in year 2. Whilst no one would claim universal validity for such results, the outcome sits well with historical beliefs.

Nevertheless most companies should forget sophisticated mathematical models and go for the "huddle".

The huddle should include the advertising agency and a key player from the client's finance function. It rarely does but it should. The objective is to bracket some believable objectives and spending plans by eliminating the impossible and the unbelievable. The scientist may scoff but rules of thumb are not that daft. Some such are:

- Last year plus inflation
- We seem to have a decent advertising campaign at last so let's give it a go. Conversely, is this campaign really doing much for us?
- Keeping up with the competition. 'Share of voice' is the equivalent in media spending to market share
- We have to hit this profit target: the advertising budget will have to give or take the slack
- Let's invest next year's money now. If it works we can do it again; if it doesn't we can skip a year

The reason a huddle works is because a cluster of forecasts in response to each strategy builds up a 'fuzzy' picture. No one can explain later **why** the targets for awareness, attitudes, sales, spending and profits are right. The fact that all the key players are comfortable with them, believe them and can commit to them is enough. Of course, it does help to ensure that the objectives are internally consistent with each other and consistent with past experience.

You may have noticed a logic problem here: how can you decide the objectives before you know the campaign? How can you decide the campaign without first setting the objectives? If you fell for that one, revisit your use of vertical thinking. Objectives in the real world are constantly revised to meet current conditions.

### The creative brief

A clear statement of objectives, or 'creative brief', is the theoretical cornerstone of new creative work. It defines the target consumer market, the positioning of the brand, and the awareness and attitude measures the brand now has and expects the advertising to provide. The fewer objectives, the better the focus for the creative team. Typically, the brief will contain supporting reasons for the consumer to buy the brand as well as background and competitive information. As an integral part of the brand plan, the agency should be involved in the wider picture.

Some believe that the briefing process should be in two or more stages: mega client (e.g. international or MD) briefs local/junior client who briefs the agency, i.e. the account team, and they in turn work out a brief for/with their creative team. Sequential briefing has merit: the account group can be more objective, the creatives more professionally motivated. Against that, sequential briefing can lose in translation; 'send reinforcements' becomes 'send three and fourpence'. On balance one brief agreed by all the relevant people in the same room at the same time is generally the way to go.

The debate which decides on the brief may be long and acrimonious. The agency, after all, is representing the consumer and needs to be convinced. Any brand has beauty spots to its owner which are warts to the agency. When the talking is done, put the brief in writing and have everyone sign, provide thumbprints, and give blood, seminal fluid or other incontrovertible genetic identification of agreement. Otherwise the new advertising will be accompanied by an even newer brief.

Why is the brief so important? Is it not easier just to judge the advertising as advertising? The theory is that a client, being long on rationality but short of more delicate sensibilities, can judge the quality of the brief but not the creative concept itself. Once a brief is agreed, the theory goes, the client should accept the agency's judgement on the creative concept provided it is in line with the brief. Not many clients accept that.

In practice both sides cheat. Roles reverse like spinning tops.

The reality is that the brief is unimportant; the process leading up to it is what matters. For the process to be effective, however, everyone has to *believe* the brief to be important – hence the signing ceremony. Time spent fighting over the brief is rarely wasted. If the frustrations of the process cause some lateral thinking and a great, but totally different, advertisement results, no experienced marketing person would be surprised.

At the end of the day remember that roles will out: agencies are in love with advertising not brands. Great and famous advertising is not necessarily good for the brand. The Typhoo gnu, Joan Collins and Cinzano, the Hovis village street and the Hennessy St Bernard were wonderful campaigns but were ultimately judged to be counter-productive.

## 4. DECISION MAKING

### *Research*

Tracking studies to measure awareness and attitudes pre and post advertising are basic good practice. So is commissioning all research independently of the agency. That excludes research the agency arranges to collect its own information or ensure its own quality control before client presentation.

A further basic principle should be the use of research to improve advertising productivity after client approval and before production. A brilliant idea can lose its shine with indifferent execution just as much as an ordinary idea can be effective with brilliant production. Historically, UK agencies were seen as more 'creative' relative to the USA but the American agencies were ahead on production values. Lately, however, there has been so much transatlantic interchange that the differences are now more cultural than professional.

Sensitive use of research at the mid-production stage will identify things which need improving. For example, cameras can track the movement of a respondent's eyes while watching an advertisement and show pupil dilation which indicates interest or attention. Surface brightness indicates attraction/repugnance. Portions of the advertisement which are shown to be 'boring' can then be improved. Some claim that results testify to the improvements obtained through the use of such technology. Others claim it is hogwash.

The key question about research is whether one researches a new campaign prior to deciding, or decides first and uses research to debug any problem areas, or hedges one's bets by accepting the campaign subject to research. Should research make the decision?

In the research chapter, the position is taken that research should be used for illumination, not support. Most professional marketers will, if funds permit, want to research a major campaign, probably first with discussion groups and then with quantitative methods. Specialist research agencies can be called in to compare the performance of new concepts against previous research of other advertising at similar stages. With that support, the marketers will make their final decision about the campaign.

That is a fine way to have safe advertising. Great advertising, if you can find it, is likely to research badly and yet provide wonderful results. To run a major advertising campaign with no research would be foolhardy, but poor results don't necessarily indicate a poor campaign. The reason is simply that the consumer, in research, responds well to the familiar. Great advertising will become familiar but as great advertising is usually also original advertising it is not familiar at the time of the research. The problem may be compounded by the lower quality of the ad during the pre-production stage as opposed to the final stage. Great campaigns take time to be recognized; good research results should be taken as a warning.

### Making the decision

In the hands off model, choosing the new campaign can be left to the agency. We will assume, though, that you have chickened out of that option. Everyone else does.

So, you have chosen the 'meddling' option, hopefully in less extreme form. Iluminated or otherwise by research, the campaign has been presented. The client team has commented in order of ascending seniority. You have noticed that everyone has said something good about the campaign and something bad. Whatever happens, they will be right. Now what? It is time for a decision, and the sheen of the long table is reflecting a dozen pairs of glinting eyes, all swivelled towards you.

You may believe that the agency should always be sent packing the first time since they can always do better if they try harder. This technique, where it works at all, has limited duration; soon, the word gets out. Some agencies even present a straw campaign the first time on principle; it makes the real one look better.

Decision-making is too subjective to define best practice. Nevertheless, there is much to be said for resisting hasty conclusions. Advertising with instant appeal may not mature well. Live with a new campaign for a few days. Put the roughs on a wall, perhaps. Agencies scoff, but taking the work back for the family to discuss is not so crazy. Then decide.

If you need the illumination of research but the total budget is so small that one has to choose between advertising and research, the office or warehouse staff will give a more realistic response than the sales force The former will tell you what they feel, while the latter will be trying to second guess customer reaction.

Advertising decisions should really be left to the consumer, not in research but in reality. One person's mature judgement, not a committee, should open the gate to media usage. A tingling sensation of acceptable risk may be that person's guiding factor. Establish the quality of the advertising before the quantity. There is a temptation to achieve awareness and attitude targets by numbers, to throw money at the problem. This is wrong. Quite soon after a campaign is launched most people will know how good it is, few, if they are honest, before. Only when the campaign has established its brilliance should you unlock the treasure chest.

Advertising works on 'highs'. The great exponents can be impatient with pedantic details such as tracking studies and creative briefs. 'Famous advertising starts here' used to be written impressively on charts, as if to deny the value of anything so pedestrian as analysis. Today's tougher relationships may be more professional, and rightly so.

The challenge is to reconcile that professionalism with the flights of fancy that create giddy patterns in the sky and capture the consumer's imagination, attention and respect. Great advertising rides as high as a kite. Feet on the ground, the string in control and yet the creative execution is pulling up and providing lift. Blue skies? Crazy? This is advertising; it should be.

- **MEMO TO FILE**

*Subject:* ADVERTISING KITE HIGH

- What kind of advertising do you need? If high visibility and impact are important, then so are a burst of creativity and a burst of spending. If your resources cannot achieve these, do not advertise.

- Advertising performance against the original objectives and the agency/client relationship should be formally reviewed once a year. Objectives should include awareness and attitudes of the target market and spending, as a minimum. Consider payment for results.

- The 'hands off' model is unlikely to be used but it is a benchmark for your own approach. The hands off model is:

  - Choose appropriate agency
  - Define comprehensive objectives in joint creative brief
  - Do not prescribe the answers
  - Run tracking studies pre and post advertising

- Recognize that defining the brief, finding the right quality of advertising and defining the quantity, or weight of spending, is an iterative process only roughly in that order because all are inter-linked. Use the 'huddle' with all the key players when those three elements have to be defined or revised. Quality is more important than quantity.

- Use research to improve advertising, not to decide it.

# B

## 2. Brand equity

**ISSUES:**

1. What is a brand? The components are the product, packaging and intangible attributes, or added values, that make up brand personality.
2. A brand is a myth but a valuable one. Building brand personality.
3. Measuring brand value or equity.
4. Brand Equity Assessment as a performance measure.
5. Brand extensions.
6. Own label policies.

### 1. WHAT IS A BRAND?

In the beginning a brand was the red hot iron used for applying a mark of ownership. The burn was indelible and difficult to imitate. Today, brand owners use holography to distinguish their products from the fakes. Techniques change, the concepts remain the same.

A 'marked man' was a criminal or slave who had been branded with a hot iron. Branding has associations with infamy that still linger. Consumerists see brands as devices for raising prices;

branding and marketing are confidence tricks. Cunning and powerful transnational corporations manipulate ordinary people, it is implied, to buy what they do not need at prices they cannot afford.

Naturally the scene when viewed from the other side looks different. It is not the mega-corporation towering over the victimized consumer, say the marketers, but the all-important consumer dictating whims and fancies to a feeble marketer.

The nature of branding lies at the root of understanding marketing: a brand is simply the promise of the bundle of attributes that someone buys and that provides satisfaction. That last word is important. It was Plato who first figured out that reality is all in the mind, and Bishop Berkeley who stated that beliefs equal realities until destroyed. As long as the consumer accepts the attributes of the brand, and enjoys the experience of using it, then that brand provides value. The attributes that make up a brand may be real or illusory, rational or emotional, tangible or invisible. A brand is a mnemonic for the consumer: it is easier to remember a single brand name than all those of different product characteristics, and easier too when trying to remember which product has which set of characteristics.

Every brand has one or more products. They may be goods or services, consumer or industrial. There is also confusion between the terms *brand* and *product*. What was once a brand manager is now called a product manager. There are a number of threads in this particular evolution, one of which is a sensitivity to the negative associations of the term *brand*. Marketers want to provide real benefits to consumers because that makes the job of selling so much easier. Products can be more clearly related to benefits than can brands.

In a way it is wrong to analyse a brand, for a consumer does not. A brand is, or should be, a single identity and no more. Nevertheless we need to be clear, so let us make the following general statement about what creates a brand:

Product + Packaging + Added values = Brand

The packaging on physical goods is apparent enough, but the

packaging that wraps around services may be obvious or invisible. Avis has to be visible to travellers in unknown airports. The fascia, uniforms, and paperwork are designed to be attention-getting but also value-adding. The packaging of a radio station, on the other hand, will be negligible, but the station will still be attempting to add value and will have an equally strong identity in the minds of its listeners.

## 2. THE BRAND AS A MYTH

The Oxford English Dictionary defines a myth as 'a traditional narrative . . . embodying popular ideas on natural or social phenomena.' Primitive cultures use myths to create a link with the large and overwhelming world around them. In ancient Greece myths helped people understand society and the workings of the human mind. Myths can never really be described as true or false, they just exist in popular culture. A limited company has no tangible reality. It is as invisible as a brand. The law, however, considers a limited company to be a legal person and treats it accordingly.

Building brands is the business of building myths. Marketers should not be over-concerned with whether it is tangible or real or substantial, or even with the true meanings of those words. Consumers want myths; they create them, enjoy them, and perpetuate them. Bronze age man, being starved of television, attributed personalities to the trees, water and rocks around him. He gave them names and fantasies. Rationally, he knew they were trees and water and rocks, but he wanted to personalize whatever he had to deal with.

A trip down a supermarket aisle is hardly the modern equivalent of dallying with Pan in some sylvan glade, but brands do have personalities. Those personalities are created by users, the consumers, as well as by marketers. When building the myth, marketers will ask consumers what they think and then try to capitalize on the more positive aspects. What consumers think may, or may not, have come from any past marketing efforts.

The idea of taking a piece of lime with Mexican beer was not originated by any brewer. Presumably the idea came from

Tequila and just meant 'Mexico' to many consumers. When Corona found Californians doing it, however, they were quick to help the word of mouth along.

The added values that turn a product into a brand are most obvious when the same product is sold under different labels. It may be worth more to one consumer than another because of the fit between the brand's identity and the consumer's self perception. Some people will buy Gucci shoes because they are Gucci; others will think they are over-priced. The brand is a bridge connecting the supplier's product with consumer acceptance.

The existence of the brand and its products are independent to some extent. Under a single brand identity, different products can come and go. Sainsbury's, to take an extreme case, sees itself as a brand and the products bearing its name as part of that.

## 3.  MEASURING BRAND EQUITY

The separation of brand from product becomes more important when considering the concept of brand equity. This is a 1980s term for the old idea that a brand has a value of its own, beyond the value that comes from the product. Brand equity is shorthand for what a brand is worth. For example, if Inter-Continental Hotels buys a suitable building from Bloggs City Centres, they will be able to charge more *and* give more satisfaction. The addition of the Inter-Continental brand name has raised the value of the business. That is one way of measuring brand equity: there are a number of others.

Brand equity became a hot topic in the 1980s because companies were being bought and sold for the value of their brand names. Rowntrees went to Nestlé, Martell to Seagram, Kentucky Fried Chicken to PepsiCo. This triggered a fierce debate in the UK about whether such values should appear on the balance sheet. Not to include brand values would under-value a company in the eyes of its shareholders and make it vulnerable. Shareholders might, in the heat of the battle, receive less than they should. Rank Hovis McDougall had their brands valued and listed them as assets.

To take a simple example, suppose company A has a net worth (or total assets less total liabilities) of £50m. It finds Company B, which may be worth anything up to £100m in terms of future earnings to Company A. After a competitive auction, Company A buys Company B for £80m. Unfortunately, it only has £20m of net assets on the balance sheet. The rest of the value is made up by some marvellous brand names.

Company A now has a choice. If it does not put the brands on its balance sheet, its net worth becomes a negative £10m (originally £50m less £80m cash plus £20m of Company B's net assets). It has therefore become insolvent while at the same time doing a marvellous deal which added £20m (£100m less £80m) to the real value of the company. If it *does* put the brands on the balance sheet then the apparent net worth will remain the same (£50m) since the net assets plus the brands will equal the cash paid out.

The example is perhaps over-simplified, but it makes the basic point. If brands are not treated as assets, the companies doing the buying have to show the borrowings on one side of the balance sheet but a gaping hole on the other. If the price being paid is largely for brands, a balance sheet would indicate that they are headed for receivership when they have just brought off a commercial coup. But why should the cost of the brands not appear on the balance sheet alongside the other acquired assets? Not only are they more important than tangible assets, they are likely to last longer.

Despite this, accountants will continue to debate whether, and if so, how brands should appear on balance sheets for years to come. The controversy has highlighted a fundamentally important concept for marketers: their function is not just to achieve short-term profits, but increase the equities of the brands in their charge. This means not only increasing the value of each brand, but developing the full width and depth of that brand's personality. Increasing value, however, is a good place to start.

A house has no objective value but only what value the market indicates, i.e. what someone will pay. There are enough properties being sold at any time to give some confidence to the arithmetic; the exceptional highs and lows can be averaged out.

Adjustments can be made for known differences such as garages or gardens. But even with all the data they have available, property valuers sometimes revert to an approach that seems circuitous to a layman : estimated rental is grossed up by the expected percentage return on investment to give the capital value which then generates the rental.

Brand valuers have essentially the same problem as property valuers but with less data. Where a brand has been purchased, the price may become the 'value' for balance sheet purposes. It may be the remainder after the other assets have been subtracted from the total purchase price for the business. Accountants generally list assets at the lower of market value and cost. An acquisition sets market value and cost initially but value will need checking thereafter.

In theory a brand's value is the capital worth of the premium it achieves over the equivalent generic product, i.e. the same thing without the brand name. The premium arises from four factors:

1. Higher price paid by customers and consumers.
2. Greater volumes
3. Greater certainty/predictability arising from consumer demand as distinct from sales push

*less* Any greater marketing expenditure required to achieve 1 – 3

There are as many as six ways to value brands, the details of which need not detain us here. There is a case for worrying less about the methodology and more about the outcomes. If three different methods and sets of assumptions yield three answers not too far apart, then anything in the middle of that triangle ought to be good enough.

## 4.  BRAND EQUITY ASSESSMENT AS A PERFORMANCE MEASURE

We are not concerned with the technicalities of balance sheets but with improving marketing performance. A healthy brand will spin off profits for many years into the future. Building a brand has less to do with sales or market share or short-term profit than with building the brand equity from which these things flow.

The concept of brand equity has not been around for long enough to allow measurement standards to emerge. In any case the exact numbers are less important than the focus away from the immediate results onto the longer horizon which brand equity requires. Let the accountants and the marketers do the arithmetic any way they want; a brand that is growing clearly has more equity than one which is not. Ninety per cent in-store distribution with increasing sales velocity beats 95 per cent and declining.

How brand equity is assessed is far less important than the fact that it is. The answers are less important than the process. Brand managers are the custodians of their company's future. Brand equity is a company's life insurance. If you want to skip the premiums, be sure you know what you are doing.

The annual Brand Equity Assessment, or whatever title it is given, should challenge the prevailing wisdom and status quo about the brand. Caesar rode in his chariot with a slave whose sole purpose was to tell him that his feet were made of clay. Consumer values shift, and a brand has to keep pace. The more scientific marketers will want more analysis of positioning for the brand and the competition, more research into the particular attributes and associations, details of the individual products, sizes, how well they are doing and how they fit. How much of this analysis is necessary and appropriate will depend on the brands, the company and the amount of money involved.

Whatever the quality of the information and analysis, the discussion has to return to the brand as a whole. Brand equity is multi-dimensional. To see it represented just by the money the brand is worth is like defining a person simply by his bank balance. Analysis of any dimension of a brand has the same limiting effect. Ultimately, one has to step back and look at the whole brand from the consumer's point of view.

To its management, a brand should be an old friend; its eccentricities and perhaps its old-worldliness can be over-looked. Acquiring the objectivity to see what outsiders see can be an effort. When all the analysis is done, there are just two questions: is the brand set far enough apart from its competitors? and is it attractive enough to the target market? These are the drivers of brand equity. We will consider them both further under 'Positioning' which is, in a sense, a set of start points for marketing. Later re-positioning adjusts the bundle of attributes, real or illusory, so that the brand can be closer to consumer preferences and still true to itself. In the annual planning cycle of most corporations, a review of brand equity should include discussion of positioning and lead to the main strategies for the brand being continued or, if necessary, amended.

However brand equity is measured, it is worth doing. Marketing managers should deliver short-term and long-term profit. How can you even consider whether short-term activities are damaging the long term without some comparative measure?

If you have no better place to start, then ask the accounting team to place a capital value on the four streams of profit/cost arising from price premium, added volume, volume reliability and marketing expenditure.

Then they can value each brand any way they like. The aim is not to find a value that will withstand audit on the balance sheet but a consistent valuation process for internal use from year to year.

Most accept that management performance is likely to improve in areas measured and highlighted. If you want your brands to increase in value, then assess brand equity at least annually.

## 5. BRAND EXTENSIONS

Attention has also focused on extensions out of the original product category of the brand. A brand of audio-tapes will evolve naturally from product to product as technology advances. The more interesting question is the extent to which the name can be applied to tape players (easy) or telephones (?).

The financial incentives to extend are considerable, especially just after a brand has been acquired. The investment has already been made and the franchise with the consumer exists. Gaining distribution is relatively simple. The odds against new brand success, reputed to be 40-1, become closer to evens if the additional product itself performs well.

The idea is not new. When Cavenham foods bought Bovril in the 1960s, Chicken Bovril appeared soon after. Heinz made a virtue of 57 varieties a generation earlier. Since the dawn of branding, equity has been maintained, and built, by moving on with new products and gracefully discarding the old as they fall out of favour.

At the same time there are risks. Too many products under the same brand name can dilute the prestige of the name. The French call it vulgarization; the Pierre Cardin name was diminished from high to low premium by excessive exposure and extension over a ten year period. Extensions can also endanger the essence of the brand. Does the addition of lemon and orange flavours to Perrier bring its fundamental purity into question?

Extensions are usually considered as new product categories at around the same relative price premium. The price of a Lacoste shirt relative to its commodity equivalent is about the same as any other Lacoste item. But when the name is licensed out to different companies, such a policy is threatened. Christian Dior suits became low-priced relative to its perfume ranges, with consequences for management action.

There is another type of extension which may be more acceptable in Hispanic and Japanese cultures than in Anglo-Saxon markets: extending upwards in price whilst remaining in the same category. Whisky marketers have found it difficult to persuade British or American drinkers to buy higher qualities within the same brand whereas Japanese expect to find a ladder of safe steps so that they can trade up and up as they become more affluent. The premium level of whisky indicates seniority. However, the portfolio that is harmonious in Japan may be less so in the USA. What is true for whisky is not true for all categories. Nescafé succeeded in persuading British consumers to trade up to Gold Blend. The product advantages were tangible. Holders of American Express cards are invited to trade up to Gold and Platinum.

Marketing, as ever, is specific to the context of country,

product category and timing. Accordingly, whilst marketers try to standardize individual products globally, the whole brand may need to remain more flexible. Selective national extensions are one way to market a brand globally whilst meeting the needs of individual markets.

### Brand Extension Policies

Marketers are clear about extension policies:

1. The new products must fit, and ideally reinforce, the brand positioning either where it is or, better still, where it is going. The brand has a relationship with the consumer. Will the extension strengthen that relationship? The quality of the extension must be at least as high as the original.

2. While quite a long stretch is possible over time, the individual steps should either be small or very occasional. New positionings in particular take time to settle. There are exceptions to this rule, but they are rare.

3. An extension should have some rationality. While not essential, positive perceptions are less likely to be disturbed if the extension makes sense. The lack of a 'reason why' is one more hazard for the product to cross.

4. Additions demand more time and effort from the sales force and everyone down the distribution chain. The effect may be to cannibalize one or more existing products or to bring new interest in the whole range. Clearly the net effect needs to be positive. It might well be the right time to prune the dead wood.

5. Either the extension is intended to become the flagship product of the brand, or the flagship needs special attention lest the novelty factor distracts the sales team from the breadwinner.

Marketers should also be clear about the risks. At the very least a brand equity assessment should be made using pessimistic forecasts.

### Testing extension skills

Extension policies are easy to agree; the problem lies with implementation. While most marketers are sure their experience can distinguish a good 'fit' for a brand extension from a bad, the evidence is that their individual responses vary markedly. The problem is further compounded by execution; a poor fit well presented within the style and personality of the brand may work better than a perfect fit clumsily introduced. Taking a brand extension to market involves participation by many managers. Harnessing combined experience, or corporate learning, should maximize its chances, but do nodding heads around a table indicate true agreement or the after-effects of a fine lunch? The subtlety and subjectivity of brand extension makes it particularly vulnerable to misleading research and false consensus.

It can be worth sensitizing management to these risks by playing an extension-testing game before any decision to extend the brand. Specialist consultants and academics will have variants of this game on computer disks, but the basics are simple enough. A set of possible extensions are created for well known brands. Each respondent is then asked, separately, to score the extension on quality of fit with the main brand and likelihood of success both as an extension and overall, i.e. the net of cannibalisation or other negative impacts on the rest of the business. Finally, the respondents are asked to identify brand extensions by competitors which have proved either beneficial or prejudicial to their businesses and say why.

The purpose of the game is simply to highlight to those concerned what the factors are and the divergencies (if any) in their separate opinions. Agreement, naturally, is no indication of being right; all it shows is that when the actual decision arrives, any apparent consensus will probably also be real.

## OWN LABEL POLICIES

Most of the discussion of the wisdom of supplying retailers' own labels, or brands, concerns marginal costing and relationships with those customers. A third factor which needs to be taken into account is the effect on brand equity. A supplier with no brands in the category has no reason to withhold own label products but may not have the expertise or the covered overheads or the relationship to worry about in the first place. Conversely a brand leader may have all the economic benefits but will at the same time have brand equity to lose.

Even if the consumer remains unaware that the retailer's label and the brand leader come from the same stable, the retail customer is inviting the brand leader to increase quality competition. The decision to supply own label may or may not be correct. It would be wise to make it, however, after first taking account of any effect of long-term competition on brand equity.

## CONCLUSION

A brand is one or more products with their packaging plus a set of intangible attributes making up the brand personality. These added values allow a brand to charge premium prices and/or make more profits than the equivalent commodities after allowing for the brand maintenance costs. To put it more simply: if you run a Brand Equity Assessment exercise and determine that the brand has little or no value, then it is not a brand.

Brand equity is a useful concept for marketers whether or not it is reported on balance sheets. The essence of a brand needs clear thinking by management and at least an annual review. The quantifiable aspects should provide some measure of longer term custodianship.

Brand equity is a measure of customer and consumer goodwill. It is a storehouse of value for the future. The test of brand extension or contraction should not just be the scale of short term profits but also the ultimate effect on brand equity.

- **MEMO TO FILE**

*Subject:* BRAND EQUITY

- The most valuable equity of a brand will arise from the mythology created by consumers. When that is available, go with the flow.

- Establish some understanding of the equity of each brand at an annual assessment meeting with year to year consistency. Brand equity cannot be fully quantified but conscious analysis will maintain balance and give better perspective on performance.

- Think about a brand's personality as a whole. Taking it to pieces all the time may not reveal the essence. Is the personality attractive and distinctive enough?

- How well do the products reinforce the brand? Are there others which could be more positive? Brand extension is not a patching job but long term alignment of a brand's personality with products which strengthen total brand equity over time.

- Think about some way of testing management consensus on brand extensions before decision-making. Review possible impact on brand equity.

# C

# 3.   Compete or cooperate?

**ISSUES:**

1. The western preoccupation with competition can be counter-productive to consumer values. Legislators and marketers need a wider understanding.
2. Cooperation is intrinsically more profitable but it must be ethical, legal and encourage growth. What forms can it take?
3. When to cooperate and when to compete.

## 1.  COMPETITION RULES IN THE WEST, BUT HOW WISELY?

The Cowboys and Indians school of economics is firmly embedded in western thinking. According to this school, consumers are good, profits are bad and industrialists are as wicked as they are allowed to be. Competition is good. More of it is better. Any gathering of industrialists is presumed to be fixing prices unless proved otherwise. American and European legislation is waist deep with measures to trap collusion; cooperative arrangements are presumed to be against consumers' interests.

That simple view does not match reality. A telephone utility, for example, sets out to connect everyone; that is its purpose. If there were as many utilities as subscribers, there would be no connections. Just one utility may be a monopoly but it meets the purpose intended: it creates a shared network. Even when there is no monopoly, cooperation may be essential; for example, computer makers cooperate over standards and consumers benefit from the ability to attach machines from one maker to those of another and to move software from PC to PC.

As each generation of management learns and shares good practices they become new conventions, an unwitting form of cooperation but valuable to marketer and consumer alike. They read the same media, take practices as they move from place to place, share forecasts and expectations. Perish the day that this book should ever be conventional wisdom! In excess, such cooperation, conscious or otherwise, develops into a club stultifying change and thereby depriving the consumer of new options. Something is needed to break it up. The question is, what?

Economic models today are either complex enough to explain whatever reality has just happened, or simple enough to be understood. Their complexity has gone beyond the wit of legislators. Legislative moves to impose competition on the marketplace create muddle and confusion.

UK brewers have long been seen by the Office of Fair Trading as having too many subtle forms of cooperation for the consumer's good. The Monopolies Commission investigations were reported in 1969 and 1989, and there were intervening lesser investigations. The 1989 report set out to introduce more competition by separating the two major sectors of the brewers' business: brewing/distribution and retailing. That simplistic goal triggered a series of negotiated fudges. In essence, the number of pubs that could be tied to the largest breweries was limited.

The brewers argued that the UK already had more competition brewing than anywhere else (true) and that there was no cause for concern (subjective). The disruption to the market through the introduction of artificial rules, they said, would lead to less competition, less choice and higher prices, the very

opposite of what was intended. One of the six authors of the
MMC report, L.A. Mills, had the vision and the courage to
submit a dissenting minority report. Mills and the brewers
proved to be correct: the imposition of artificial structures to
increase competition has actually reduced it. Both the retail
industry and the breweries have consolidated. A more striking
example comes from the US airline industry. In 1978 there were
21 major airlines but only eight shared 82 per cent of the total
business. Prices were deemed high and marketing practices
uncompetitive. The industry was seen as a club. Cooperation
was seen as against the consumer interest. Action had to be
taken.

Deregulation encouraged more airlines to be created and
existing ones to expand. There was more choice and prices fell.
Planes, loaded with consumers, also spent more time waiting to
take off or circling to land. Consumers enjoyed the reduced
prices, but not the reduced services.

Fourteen years on, what has been achieved? Of the 21 airlines,
only seven are now not in some form of bankruptcy. Those
seven have virtually the entire market. Prices can be expected
to escalate now that the weak have gone to the wall. Consumer
choice and competition are sharply down. Few would argue that
the old club needed breaking up. At the same time, deregulation
as it came about has lost much of the intended benefit. Both
government and airlines would have benefited from a more
sophisticated vision of the advantages of limited competition
within wider cooperation.

OPEC has had only sporadic success in its attempts to form
producers into a cartel. Some see it as a device to keep prices
artificially high. Others view it as a means of maintaining some
stability, to the benefit of all. Moving downstream, the main oil
companies raise or lower UK prices with remarkable unanimity.
One company will move and the others match immediately. Is
this competition or cooperation? Are UK prices excessively
high? In the 1980s, supermarkets saw petrol retailing as a
valuable addition to the car parking space they increasingly
provided. By the end of the decade, their market share had
crept towards seven per cent. In early 1992 their prices averaged

10 to 15 pence per gallon below the oil companies' own retail outlets. Some expect their market share to grow to 30 per cent by the end of the decade, particularly if the government policy to remove car and petrol tax perks proves successful. Will the oil companies allow such a price shift from their own stations? Expect a Monopolies Commission enquiry within the decade.

The immediate lesson is that artificial imposition of competition does not necessarily benefit the consumer. Benefits from de-nationalization (telephones, steel, gas and so on) have less to do with the creation of competition than with the introduction of decent management, responsive to the consumer. There *is* compelling evidence which suggests that a market-oriented business will prove more successful than those with other agenda. The interests of marketers and consumers have to be compatible because marketers recognize the primacy of the consumer. Competition is not necessarily a benefit to the consumer; choice is. And, depending on the circumstances, choice and value for money may be better from a monopoly than from any number of competitors.

There is little point in trying to demonstrate that oil companies do or do not compete. The reality is that they both compete and cooperate. Tracking prices is very little guide to whether their behaviour is truly benefiting consumers or not.

Some cynics believe that a market orientation means turning the market over to orientals. Eastern countries do indeed have a sophisticated understanding of marketplaces and the benefits of cooperation over competition. Centuries of experience have inculcated team cultures; by putting shared advantage before individual gain, greater results can be achieved. Of course this analysis is superficial, but you do not need to be a genius to figure out that cooperative behaviour is more likely to be profitable than competitive.

## 2. COOPERATION IS MORE PROFITABLE

Rosabeth Moss Kanter, in *When Giants Learned to Dance*, reviewed the performance of corporations where the individual businesses (SBUs) were encouraged to compete with one another compared with those where they were encouraged to cooperate. The cooperators were more profitable. What is more surprising is that there are any chief executives who pull businesses into a single group and then pretend that the group does not exist. Arms-length trading is deemed to be good and healthy because it reflects the economic model of the market. Spare a thought for poor old IBM, going down this very track.

Moss Kanter concludes that cooperation is good, i.e. more profitable, when businesses share common ownership, but not otherwise. Could this be culture talking? Cooperation in the same group is legal though even that had to be tested in a US court. Imagine having a judge decide if one is allowed to cooperate with oneself!

Let us try to look at the matter logically. If companies A and B recognize that they will make more money by cooperating, then they will seek to do so. If they are part of the same group they may have other agendas or there may be artificial internal pricing rules which get in the way. If they are not part of the same group, then the lawyers will want to take a close look at the form of cooperation. Legitimizing this source of increased profitability lies at the root of modern merger and alliance activity; what is not legal between independent companies is valid for sibling companies. Thus legislation against collusion promotes greater collusion. Why does the consumer gain from forcing companies A and B into the same group? Will future innovation be enhanced?

Ground rules for approving corporate mergers and acquisitions defy rationality. Different administrations have different methods. One uses formulae to calculate industry concentration; the more a market is controlled by a few players, the less likely a new alliance will be accepted. That is a reasonable premise if only one could agree the 'market'. Another is used by the US authorities. They multiply together the two market shares and see if the result exceeds some magic threshold. For example, two companies with shares of 20 per cent would achieve an immediate share of 40 per cent but an index of 400, which is likely to be over the threshold. Two companies with 10 per cent would merge to a 20 per cent market share business, but the score of 100 would not usually trigger a refusal. The multiplication concept is a neat way to highlight excessive market share, usually only one factor in the review process.

Irrationality arises from the subjectivity in choosing the 'market' in which share is calculated; which territory and which product category figures should be used. Are we considering the UK or the EC or the world? The global market has arrived; does it make sense to consider anything less? If this is a merger between two salad dressing companies, are we considering salad dressings or savoury cold food accompaniments? Do we include vinegar, which is used for other purposes, and how many oils are relevant?

Price levels also define markets. Does champagne compete with sparkling wine? It does and it doesn't. To draw a line arbitrarily to exclude or include sparkling wine makes no sense. Usage also defines markets. When Johnson & Johnson found adults using their baby powder, they redefined their market. Ted Leavitt memorably pointed out that failure to identify the market would lead to corporate failure. The nub is that the definition of 'market' is a matter of personal choice, not a foundation stone on which to legislate or build businesses.

A brand is a bundle of attributes, some tangible, some not. Some are presented to the consumer as competitive with other brands; the rest, *de facto*, are forms of cooperation. This does not necessarily damage consumer interests. Airlines do not compete with one another on safety: the consumer expects and deserves the highest standards from them all. If they can help each other be safer, so much the better. The line between areas for cooperation and competition will be redrawn from time to time. The objective here is not to challenge consumer rights or the need for something more than buying power for protecting those rights. Marketers should recognize to the importance of cooperation over competition, and legislators need to take more intelligent longer term views.

## 3.  WHEN TO COOPERATE AND WHEN TO COMPETE

The fallacies embraced by regulators are shared by too many

marketers. The competition-is-good-but-cooperation-is-naughty culture is widespread. Competition is important, but it is not all it is cracked up to be. Market, or any other share, should not dominate thinking. Marketing is not a zero sum game*; all can win, including consumers, or all can lose. The conventional wisdom that market share is also an index of profitability has some academic credibility but the evidence is not strong. At the end of the day, the consumer wants value for money and the marketer wants profit. Achieving both at the same time is the objective, what anyone else is achieving is secondary. Indeed if your competitor is increasingly successful, he has every reason to leave you alone.

None of these cooperation versus competition issues can be taken to extremes, but it is worth considering how to make your competitor more successful if that will lead to your own success. Were the US airlines smart to approach deregulation the way they did? On balance those who precipitated excessive competition were also the losers. At the other extreme, a competitor that becomes too successful may stamp on your business and hardly notice.

Oddly enough, the more competitive a market is the less you have to worry about competition. Where a market has only two competitors, such as detergents in many markets or Coke and Pepsi, market share does indeed become a preoccupation. For a company with only one competitor, forecasting the response to any move becomes more important. Secrecy becomes more vital. The possible retaliations are fewer and are possible to estimate. But, when many businesses compete, no one business is critical to another, the possibilities are too many to calculate and the need to respond is less urgent. Obviously that generalization is only true within limits; any major move that is generally threatening should have anticipated the responses.

Excessive concern with competition leads to poor marketing. It can dissipate creativity and shift attention away from consumers and customers. Matching competitive advertising weights is

---

*A zero sum game is one where the total gains made by players equals the total losses by the others. The total of wins and losses is always zero.

likely to be wasteful. Copycat brands, 'me-toos', take up space, energy and financing. The consumer benefit is price which may, or may not, be worthwhile.

Oriental thinking has long recognized that one should only compete or do battle when one can do so decisively. Opportunities for doing so will be rare. Most of the time one should either cooperate or stay out of the way. Differentiation is one way of avoiding competition; not only does it give the customer a reason to buy, it provides a reason for the competitor not to be alarmed. The more different your product is seen to be, the less of a threat it will pose.

This can be a major factor for a new brand. When Aqua Libra was introduced to the UK in 1987, GrandMet maximized brand differentiation. The lower its profile, the smaller the niche it appeared to fit, the more eccentric, the less there was for competition to worry about. In turn, the less waste and extragavance GrandMet had to give the launch. Given their tiny involvement in carbonated drinks, Aqua Libra was vulnerable. The brand was positioned to stay as far away from competition as possible. Ferrero Rocher in chocolates, and many other premium brands, have followed the same strategy.

Product and brand differentiation is not the only way to avoid competition but it is a start. The next step is to conduct a competitor analysis. This is tough to do in-house. SWOT (strengths, weaknesses, opportunities and threats) analyses have the advantage of focusing management on competition but there is often a high degree of subjectivity in the comparisons. In the case of a brand, a third party, can, with the help of insiders, establish the **dimensions** along which competition, neutrality or cooperation takes place. 'Dimensions' include price, product quality, packaging and as many attributes as management find helpful. The list should be comprehensive. The same principles apply to business unit or corporate competitor analysis but the increasing complexity makes for confusion. A typical portfolio will include both stronger and weaker, cheaper and more expensive brands. Then they can estimate, objectivity being more important than precision, the **strength** of each competitor. The advertising agency can do this for most dimensions except advertising. A major brands company persuaded the editor of the leading trade magazine to provide a SWOT analysis no doubt in return for increased advertising.

When such a presentation is made, the internal team may well dispute the views of the assessor. This is where some competitive reviews fall down. Conversation develops along these lines: competitors have their strengths, we have ours, some are real, some are just perceptions, it is a mistake to imitate them less well, let's build on our own strengths and that is what we are doing anyway. Such reasoning is circular. Much of the problem arises from the presumption that the name of the game is competition. Next time you do a competitive analysis call it a 'cooperative analysis'. The process is similar but first mark out the areas of cooperation and neutrality, for those are going to provide your profits. Only then turn to competition. The areas should be both small and significant. They need to be small because, unless you are a very big company, they have to be where you can win, and win decisively.

SWOT analysis may just feed back to management what you already know. If it or any other form of competitive analysis works for your business, stay with it. Otherwise consider using 'cooperative analysis' to provide a short list of areas for cooperation and a shorter one for competition.

How can cooperation take place if it is illegal? The advice not to get caught is wrong. Companies should establish legal and ethical policies and see that they are enforced. One solution lies in 'competitive signalling'. Would you like to increase prices? An article in the trade press indicating that a price increase may be overdue can flag an intention both legitimately and without commercial risk. As a general rule, whatever takes place openly and publicly is legitimate; English law broadly accepts that purchases made in outdoor markets during daylight hours are deemed to be honestly bought.

The trade press is ostensibly a means whereby suppliers communicate with customers. A more important role is to allow suppliers to communicate with other suppliers. One can signal market trends, new products, successes and failures as well as pricing intentions. What are the future threats to the market?

What government intervention looms? Writing about these is a legitimate form of cooperation.

Another form of legitimate collusion is the alliance or joint venture. Confusion over the relevant territories and product categories, as noted above, has created a grey area which can be exploited by the formation of declared alliances. Whether they are formal or informal, open declaration of alliances to the rule-makers usually gains their approval. Recession and a shrinking globe are bringing more and more such alliances into being.

An example of the strength of outward competition within internal cooperation has been the post-war economic performance of Japan. While paying lip service to the western virtues of competition, the reality has been an unwritten set of cooperative practices. That the web tying government to the large trading houses and conglomerates *(keiretsu)*, the banks, the manufacturers and the small suppliers baffles explanation is not the point. The essence of what is now called 'neo-capitalism' is the recognition that cooperation is the essence of profit. Competition is important but can be conducted within focused areas. Prices in Japan are high but it would be hard to maintain that Japanese consumers have suffered long-term damage.

- **MEMO TO FILE**

*Subject:* COMPETE OR COOPERATE?

- Do not be preoccupied by competition. Share of market, or anything else, can be a useful statistic, but it is a secondary one because marketing is not a zero sum game. The primary objective is for the consumer to gain better value while the marketer achieves better profitability. If the competition does so too, is that a problem?

- In any case, 'market' is defined by you, not the consumer. Are you sure you have it right?

- Do not be lulled by competition. Keep the initiative through conscious 'cooperative analysis'. Make sure you compete and cooperate where you want to. Both for each brand and the company as a whole, determine all the potential areas for cooperation and competition. Then choose your weapons with care.

- If you have only one or two competitors, then give competitive intelligence a higher priority.

- Cooperation is more profitable than competition but it must be legitimate and ethical. Key methods are: product/brand differentiation, competitive signalling and alliances. Consider the use of cooperative rather than competitive analysis.

- Competition is wasteful unless it is decisive. Anticipate responses and get your retaliation in first.

# 4. Distribution channels

**ISSUES:**

1. Channels are changing to follow the consumer. They are tied to segmentation, not geographic regions.
2. Disintermediation : the number of steps in the process are getting fewer. Consumers are taking over from retailers.
3. Critical mass.
4. Channels are for information as well as product but they do not have to be the same.
5. Managing distributors.

*Figure 2    Distribution channels*

## 1. CHANNELS

The term 'channels' for distribution is well chosen. When business tides are high, any channel will do. But beneath the surface, the shifting of invisible sands may well have changed the safe route to the market. It is easy to be left high and dry when tides recess.

The links between supplier and distributor can make their partnership seem as integral as marriage, or it can be as casual as an annual order and invoice. A distributor is not just an outlet but a partner. Classically, a major supplier/distributor partnership involves emotional bonding at many levels. Such relationships, built up over many years, can be destroyed in a month when economic realities reveal changed patterns of trade.

Where brands are complex or high image, major distributors will be expected to contribute much more than their basic economic functions of breaking bulk and reselling. A major distributor creates and executes the local marketing plan as part of the whole. Local knowledge of the marketplace is referred back to be integrated into the total marketing plan.

In 1980 there were many wine and spirit distributors in California. In 1990 there were effectively only three. Why? Historically, California had been treated as three regions: north, south and the inland valley. Each area had its own set of wholesalers trading with the US importers and manufacturers. Three events then occurred: retailers merged to form state-wide chains, the US wine and spirit trade consolidated at the supplier level, and California removed its 'fair trade' legislation which set minimum margins for retailers.

of each brand to pitch for their business on an all or nothing basis, effectively shutting out all but the largest wholesalers. They passed on the resulting discounts to consumers in order to undercut their own retail competitors.

Consumers were impressed by the value for money now available from the chain stores and, subsequently, from the price clubs. Armed with the appropriate plastic card for their price club, any consumer could buy the brand leaders at low, low prices. Driving miles to get this benefit seemed not to bother many Californians: home to a Southern Californian is a place on the freeway.

Consumers and retailers were happy enough but distributors and suppliers were not. The old money-go-round went into gear again. Suppliers appointed single, state-wide distributors. The smaller fry were bought out or became irrelevant. Prices soon came back to normal, consistent levels.

This example from the wine and spirit industry does not have universal application because the numbers and roles of intermediaries between brand owner and consumer vary by product category and country. Some are simply customers buying and re-selling. Others undertake marketing activities and/or packaging and/or break bulk.

Even so, there are four trends in distribution which are all illustrated by this example:

1. Consolidation by retailers and brand owners forces those in between – the distributors – to consolidate or quit.
2. Road and other transportation links are improving. Information flows are becoming much faster. Both these forms of improved communications shorten the effective distance from brand owner to consumer, and allow the number of links in the distribution chain to be reduced. The fancy name for this is 'disintermediation'. Bypassing one's own customers is a delicate business not usually trumpeted in advance, but the benefits of information technology and improved inventory control include less stock sitting on shelves, less out of date or stale product, less double handling and better prices for the brand owner and/or consumer. A further benefit can be the quality of information for the brand owner, of which more later.
3. Brand owners integrate forward (i.e., towards the consumer) in order to control consumer pricing. Europe in 1992 has seen great strides towards ownership by the big brand companies of their distribution systems across the whole EC, so that distributors cannot disrupt prices in other countries. Few developed countries still permit brand owners to enforce retail price maintenance, but the stronger and more consistent the line to the retailer is, the more consistent the

consumer price will be.

At the same time some retailers have integrated backwards; supermarkets in particular have taken distribution control away from manufacturers. Even where these retailers do not use in-house distribution, distributors are becoming captive.

4. Perhaps the most subtle trend is the shift created by increased leisure time and changing consumer values. Some believe that the greatest contribution to business productivity has not been motor vehicles or aircraft or mechanization/automation or computers, but self-service. Self-service doesn't just mean pumping your own petrol or collecting your own food from the counter; IKEA successfully gets people to assemble furniture themselves. The consumer enjoys taking on DIY projects or taking over the services of selection and delivery which the retailer once provided. It has changed the shape of retailing. Traditional banking was surprised that customers would rather stand in the rain to take cash from the machine in the wall than wait in line to be ignored by the clerk behind the counter. Whether the aggregate shopping time has increased or not, the patterns have changed.

The car is a factor. So are cultural shifts of values, such as more men shopping, husbands and wives both working, flexible hours, and work locations.


## 2.  DISINTERMEDIATION

The increase in discretionary spending power is less significant than greater discretionary use of time. The market responds to this in two ways: the variety of retail opportunities increases to suit consumer convenience, and the chain can be shortened to allow consumers to serve themselves. The former represents horizontal variety and the latter represents vertical variety. The market itself becomes both wider and shallower.

Today, shopping is possible seven days a week and 24 hours a day. Personal shopping is supplemented by every other medium. In a hotel, you may have to penetrate a shopping arcade to get to the bar. Duty free shopping exploits not so much the duty the customer may be saving as the time he has available in the airport or in flight.

When the consumer visits a price club or cash-and-carry, she is using her time, which may have no price ticket, to replace a retailer's time, which has. New electronic links allow consumers access further up the distribution chain if they are prepared to invest the time and trouble. Generally speaking, marketing allows consumers to trade money for time.

## 3.  CRITICAL MASS

All four trends in distribution affect brand owners. As traditional channels consolidate, new ones open up. At the same time some of the traditional decision areas for the brand owner remain:

- Should one choose a smaller specialist distribution house or a larger generalist?
- How much control over a distributor is necessary or wise?
- How much mutual dependency should exist, i.e. how much control should the distributor be allowed over the supplier?
- To what extent is it desirable to bypass middlemen and deal directly with retailers?

At the root of these issues lies the concept of 'critical mass'. This is defined in terms of a brand portfolio rather than a single brand. A portfolio with critical mass has enough clout with the customer to gain respect, or at least serious attention. When all the major UK brewers had their own soft drink ranges they had distribution in their own pubs but little in the retail chains. They did not have critical mass. Putting Coca-Cola in the portfolio, as one of them did, transformed its strength. Critical mass gains access to major buyers.

Critical mass applies at all levels of the trade down to and including retailers. Working distribution channels effectively requires both supplier push and consumer pull.

Critical mass is the threshold of power for the supplier. Below this threshold there is no power. Above it, there is the opportunity for constructive partnerships or for time-wasting positional plays. In the UK, the increasing power of the top retailers has weakened the bargaining strength of suppliers. In the high volume categories, retailers may only need the brand leaders and their own labels or own brands. Retailer power, however, has been created in part through the provision of ever larger shopping spaces with ever wider ranges to fill the ever wider shelves. This has led some stores to make it easier for small suppliers in some categories to fill specialist needs at the same time as mainstream suppliers are finding it more difficult. No one ever said it was simple.

## 4.  INFORMATION

Running silently through all these issues is the need for information. Distribution is one of the basic four Ps of marketing: place. It is critical to know where the consumer is and is going to be. The channel has to finish where the consumer is and then present the brand in the best possible way. With electronic point of sale, or point of purchase, cash registers, the retailer collects huge volumes of data on each brand including when it was sold and the price paid. Through syndicated services, higher levels of the distribution chain can access the same data.

The idea that a producer can cope with information about every transaction concerning his brand all over the world is absurd. Some means of reducing the data to human proportions is essential. The point is that information no longer has to run through the same channels as the product. Double handling information is as wasteful as carrying boxes. Key facts, by default or intent, are likely to go missing.

When reviewing distribution channels for brands, it is worth making a parallel consideration of information. How does information get from consumer to brand owner? How could it do so better, faster, cheaper? How can market information be enriched?

The idea that the distribution database is fully open to the brand owner may strike both with equal terror. Mutual dependency needs to be matched by some trust in sharing information before it has been excessively processed. The distributor needs to know what is coming from the brand owner almost as much as the brand owner needs the plain unvarnished facts of the marketplace.

The role of the distributor is far more than just that of a merchant forming one of the links between consumer and brand owner. Whether fully independent or a subsidiary of the supplier, the distributor has separate objectives. He has his own margins to worry about, his own costs, and his own goals; he also has competing distributors to worry about. Because the distributor is neither producing or selling the products, his only way to profit is to turn over the highest possible volume at the lowest possible cost. This may not fit with the product strategy for either the producer or the customer. And yet the distributor may be entrusted with a large part of the marketing effort. For this reason the traditional relationship is based on territorial separation at the national or wholesale levels: one distributor deals with one market.

Changing consumer buying patterns and increasing distributor consolidation are altering that relationship. A distributor may have more clout with traditional retailers but specialists, duty free shops for example, may need separate attention. A large part of a distributor's role is service, and new retail sectors can be penetrated through distributors already servicing those outlets. Increasing retailer sophistication in some sectors is reducing distributors' traditional clout; in the new car business, distributors are now little more than transportation experts.

Friction may develop as soon as more than one distributor services one marketplace. Partitions between customer groups, as was clear in California, are eroded by the customers themselves. Whether or not this results in further distributor consolidation, their role is reduced.

## 5. MANAGING DISTRIBUTORS

Evaluating distribution performance is as subjective as any other personal appraisal. One's own hirings may have halos whereas those one inherits have more apparent failings. Fellow subsidiaries of the same organization can be especially unattractive, since they have little dependency on the international brand manager. Large corporations, with hired hands coming and going, have a bigger problem in this area than family businesses where the relationships can succeed through generations of friendship. Multi-level contacts between suppliers and distributors are the norm, not least in order to maintain continuity.

Managing distribution channels calls for considerable understanding of marketing, marketplace information and interpersonal skills. These take time to build and should rarely be thrown away. At the same time, recognition of the developing trends in distribution require that channels be seriously reviewed on a regular basis. Performance may be fine but if retailer and consumer purchasing habits are shifting the sands, new channels may have to be cut.

- **MEMO TO FILE**

*Subject:* DISTRIBUTION CHANNELS

- Distribution channels are reducing in depth but increasing in width. The number of steps to the consumer is reducing but the consumer's retail options are increasing. So is a brand's likelihood of being stranded.

- Consider, when reviewing channels, three issues separately: physical transportation, information flows and allocation of the components of the marketing mix, i.e. who decides prices, advertising, packaging, promotions.

- Ensure that each level of the distribution chain has critical mass with the next level down. Conversely, ensure it is not dominated by the next level down.

- Whether distributors are within the same group or independent, treat them equally as partners. One day terminal decisions may be needed but, until then, the interdependency needs to be optimized. The relevance of channels to retailer and consumer needs requires at least annual review.

$$\boxed{\text{E}}$$

# 5.  Entropy is here to stay

**ISSUE:**

1.  How should a large marketing organization be structured?

Entropy is the natural state of disorder; physicists get excited about it. The rest of us take it for granted. Entropy is the condition of my desk, most organizations, their customers' businesses and their consumers' minds. Why do people expect things to be tidy? Why do they spend so much time cleaning up? (Joan Rivers once said she hated housework; you clean up and next year you have to start all over again). Where did this passion for tidiness come from?

Undoubtedly some order is necessary to get things done; enough, but not too much. In marketing, there is no evidence that the most analytic, structured, orderly marketing plans produce the best profits. Some UK research shows that companies without marketing plans are slightly more profitable than those with.

The right balance between order and disorder in any household or business is too subjective to discuss here except in one respect: what implication does entropy have for the structure of large businesses? The success of a large business depends on how it is divided into units, how well each works and how they work together.

Success is created at the border of a business. A sale is only a sale when an outsider buys something; an internal sale is not. Corporate swindlers such as Robert Maxwell survive from year to year through representing internal sales as external. A business unit can be seen as having two components: the things at the border and everything internally. It is the activities at the border which create profit. The internal activities are, by definition, invisible to customers. They may be critical to achieving sales, but they are only costs.

As a rule of thumb, a company should be more relaxed about taking on another salesman than another analyst. The first one should directly increase sales. The other may do so, but only indirectly.

In practice, companies do not organize themselves this way nor do they take on salesmen more easily than analysts. If anything, it is the other way about: an analyst will be hired to calculate whether another salesman is needed.

Activities can best be seen as flows of information. Products may be washing about as well, but the challenge of organization is to optimize the people costs. These can be modelled accurately by charting information flows.

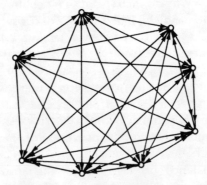

*Figure 3   Communication flows in an eight-person unit (28 lines)*

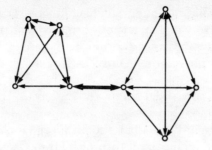

*Figure 4    Two four-person units (13 lines)*

When structuring a large organization, managers should be seeking to optimize the placement of internal borders, so that the internal costs or information flows are the least that the ideal border transactions need. This is where we finally get to the point: other things being equal, the laws of physics tell us that smaller is better than bigger.

Remember the saying from the early 70s, 'small is beautiful'? If one assumes that everyone inside the border talks with everyone else and only the border people talk to outsiders, then the number of internal information flows increases factorially (or exponentially, or a sight faster than the number of people). That is why big meetings are so unpopular.

The second law of thermodynamics says that the entropy of an isolated system always increases. Furthermore, when two systems join together, the combined entropy is greater than the sum of their individual entropies. Businessmen recognize that the shambles inherent in any two businesses is much worse when you put them together. A system left to its own devices runs down, but merging two such systems is worse. The bringing together of the UK regional railway companies in 1948 is a fine example of combined entropy.

Entropy has frequently been overlooked when explaining why acquisitions fail and why large organizations fall apart. The armed forces on the other hand, are all too familiar with the experience that the larger the numbers involved in an exercise, the more cosmic the bungle is likely to be. Don't blame the generals for every defeat; entropy is more frequently the cause. Tidiness decays because disorder is natural. The larger the organization the more nature helps to ensure disorder proliferates.

Success in any field depends on focus, good internal communications and organization. Teamwork depends on trust and other human factors but also on sheer numbers. Some say the perfect committee size is three, with two off sick. Others that 100 or 200 or 500 is the perfect number of people in a business unit. Arbitrary figures are just that: arbitrary, and what is 'small' is open for debate. But whatever scale you use, small is organizationally more attractive than big.

Entropy, i.e. disorder, is minimized by having the largest possible number of strategic business units (SBUs) as in IBM's recent reorganization. What actually constitutes an SBU is a matter for discussion. In theory, it is a unit of the business that is self-sufficient and could operate without the parent company, something a lot of SBUs dream about. That implies that each SBU must be commercially and economically viable. An SBU is a marketing organization with the resources and authority to achieve its objectives. In reality, the distinction cannot be precise. Some functions can be delegated to SBUs but some have to be shared at group level. Even so, the concept is robust enough to be used to structure organizations not only in all large businesses, but also in the armed forces, and in health and education.

What we have not yet allowed for is that these SBUs are themselves particles, so to speak, in the group's space. The more SBUs there are, the more entropy will exist at this level. In other words, the teamwork within each SBU is terrific but the SBUs may be getting on so badly with each other that the group is falling apart. Bird's Eye used to have a meat division, a fish division, and a vegetable division. What kind of problems would they have had in launching a paella ? Any system of order suppresses thought. Maybe regular reorganization is part of the solution, but then such preoccupations become part of the problem.

If market researchers are allowed to add two awareness numbers to create a mythical measure called 'total awareness', we can do the same with entropy. The 'total entropy' of a large organisation is therefore the sum of the entropies **within** each SBU **plus** the entropy **between** SBUs. Minimize total entropy and your organization is well ordered. What could be simpler?

- **MEMO TO FILE**

*Subject:* ENTROPY IS HERE TO STAY

- Entropy, the state of disorder, is natural. Focus your efforts on putting order only where it matters for results.

- A large business should organize itself into the number of SBUs that minimizes total entropy, provided that no SBU is smaller than can be economically justified. Each SBU should be a marketing organization with whatever it takes to grow success.

- Disperse staff units to SBUs to help them look outwards to the market, not inwards to HQ.

# 6. Failures bring success

**ISSUE:**

1. Recognition of the importance of failures to corporate learning. Ways to benefit.

Managers in some companies regard failure the way a rodent is petrified by a snake. As a result, immobility guarantees the very result they want to avoid. Do not blame the individual; the fault lies with corporate culture.

Their different treatment of failure is one area where Japanese culture gives its marketers such a start over westerners. They see failure as an instructive step towards success. Failure is not shaming or something to be buried with unseemly haste. The cushioning carpets of western offices, on the other hand, is not due to the generosity of Personnel Services but the amount of mistakes swept underneath.

Toshiba launches more failures than its US competitors launch products in total. Each failure is a prize to be taken back into the company and analysed for the reasons. The whole total quality movement stems from this enthusiasm for tracking errors back to their sources. Try that in the UK and fingers will point in every direction but their owners. Pointing fingers miss the point. The process that caused the error needs the correction, not the blame. The Christian church latched onto the concept of being against sin, but in favour of sinners, 1,500 years ago. Maybe we lost it with the Puritan age of intolerance.

Whatever the history, failure has become a dirty word. It is recognized by educators as the key to learning, yet some teachers compound the cultural problem by trying to protect children from failure. The sense of failure, we are told, leaves deep and indelible emotional scars. It is impossible to fail some examinations; the worst possible result is to pass with an E grade. No wonder young marketers have difficulties. To reach such eminence they have been outstandingly successful in a class where failure is unknown. Now they want to try things in order to learn and to gain experience. They are impatient with their predecessors when they say the new ideas have been tried and failed or fall outside corporate acceptability. Is not marketing the business of continual controlled innovation? Then comes the threat: 'Yes, you can try it if you insist, but be sure it will succeed before you do.'

Wiser educators and managers distinguish between small failures and large ones. An infant learns about height by falling off a chair. Falling out of a window may be more instructive but does not lead to much. Toshiba launches many products. For one of them to fail in the market is no more than falling off the chair. A western company, in the effort not to fail at all, may research a product long past the optimal launch date. The eventual launch falls out of the window.

Creating the environment where small failures are encouraged in order to provide the raw material for success means more than just fixing the culture. Business practices need to be changed too. Experimentation has to be made possible. In the ice cream business, trying a new product out in the market should be easy. If the business cannot handle small scale production for testing, it should. At the other extreme, Boeing will not build new aircraft for young managers to play with. Experimentation has to take other forms. Creative organizations make space for failures with low penalties and each achieves it in a way compatible with the business.

In the 60s, IDV discerned that UK consumers admired sherry that was pale and dry but actually preferred it to be sweet. Croft Original was born and succeeded. One good brand deserves another and the same logic was applied to table wine: consumers admired red but drank sweet. No sweet red table wine existed in any volume. Docura was created, researched well and proved an instant disaster in the market. The failure was analysed with the conclusion that the source, Portugal, was a mistake and that the tannin content was excessive: it clashed with the sweetness. Two years on, a red Hungarian wine, St Stefan, was launched. A better liquid, the pack and the source were wrong. It was not just any red wine that consumers admired: French was the thing. The late 70s saw Pierre Picard, a Vin de Pays made with special dispensation from the French authorities to allow sweetening with grape must (juice). Sugar is not allowed. Still too much tannin. Finally Le Piat d'Or hit the jackpot and became far the most successful table wine in the UK.

Once eventual success is achieved, the stepping stones of failure acquire nostalgia, even affection. In hindsight their value is obvious. What about beforehand? Enthusiasm for failure can be overdone. Most failures are genuine, authentic mistakes with no redeeming values. How do we distinguish pearls from purlers?

The value of a mistake is the amount it adds to corporate knowledge. If the corporation has already spent a small fortune to discover that square balls do not roll, allowing a new manager to make square balls will not win any prizes for leadership. Few companies are able to distinguish what they really know for certain from their collective prejudices. If you want to be a maverick, do it first but have the rationale ready.

Here is the all-purpose rationale:

1. The concept should have worked. It was essentially feasible.
2. The scale of the experiment was as small as possible.
3. There are enough profits elsewhere to hide this loss.
4. It will lead to significant additional profits. This reverse only postpones success.
5. What we have learned from this failure makes success now more likely.

If they still throw you out, be grateful. You are working for the wrong company.

Is this subversion in jest? Partly. The rationale for failure is real enough but it should not be a solo activity. As again is apparent from Japanese successes, the process needs to be collaborative. The value of failure lies in its subsequent assessment: the collaborative addition to corporate knowledge.

Some say that the only failure is the failure to try, but reality is more subtle than that. Maintaining standards, doing things as well as the organization knows how, are basic business skills. Sloppy work deserves no excuse. Encouraging well directed failure is not permissiveness, and is certainly not a deviation from clear focus on skills and objectives. It is a determination to build on those skills i.e. the corporate knowledge built up from failures.

If an organization does not have a failure culture, what can it do? Suddenly to preach the virtues of failure may not be believed, or lead to some remarkable disasters if it is. Announcing a policy of approved failure and sacking the first manager who fails, may be recognizable organization behaviour but business schools advise against that sort of thing. Changing culture head-on is itself as likely to fail as not. Changing reward systems (i.e. what triggers bonuses) has a better track record.

It is easy to welcome failures in theory but they are uncomfortable. What can one do in practice? The informal lunch is one route. The value of the 'Educated Lunch' is discussed in another chapter. The CEO who is prepared to break bread with her juniors and swap failure stories has already cracked the problem. Any CEO is bound to have had more failures, and with any luck more amusing ones, than junior marketers. The steps from talking to learning are not so great. What is a top manager if not a teacher?

The recognition of the importance of failures to learning and ultimate success is more than just the encouragement of experimentation. To try is not enough; what is learned from the trial is what matters.

Marketing is not just an analytical science. Any successful marketer will acknowledge the significance of luck. What distinguishes the successful is that they gave luck a better chance to happen. Excessive research, long delays and bureaucracy reduce the opportunity for luck to strike.

The faster the plan → experiment → measure → corporate learning → plan loop cycles round, the more often luck gets a chance. Napoleon did not want clever generals, he wanted lucky ones. The lucky ones are those prepared to risk failure.

- **MEMO TO FILE**

*Subject:* FAILURES BRING SUCCESS

- Failure goes with experimentation which is essential to progress. Encourage the small failures that lead to great successes. Otherwise fear of failure will lead to 'analysis paralysis'.

- Ensure that experimentation is directionally right and that failure will add to corporate knowledge. All existing knowledge should be brought to bear before a trial. Do not waste it.

- Marketing success ultimately is a matter of luck. Frequent experimentation gives luck the best chance.

# G

# 7. Global marketing

**ISSUES:**

1. Multinationals are going global. Why? Are they right?
2. Global marketing may provide more effective segmentation than national boundaries.
3. Success is driven by profits or structure than culture and information systems. Going global requires intensive corporate learning.

## 1. GOING GLOBAL

Does it pay to be global? Not necessarily.

Global marketing became an issue from the time Ted Levitt published *The Globalization of Markets* in 1983. His point was that people around the world were more alike than different. Modern communications were increasing universality. The world was becoming a global village. Marketers would make more money, he claimed, by concentrating on the similarities and forgetting the differences.

Outside the high tech industries, this was not the general experience and other gurus were quick to react. (For an analysis of the genus 'guru', see page 82). Philip Kotler argued that marketing was all *about* differentiation, distinguishing consumers' needs and your brand in such a way that value and profits could be established. To ignore differences would ignore the very roots of marketing. Companies needed to see things in multi-national, or better still, multi-local terms. Coca-Cola wrote to agree with Kotler. Yet in 1992, Peter Sealey, Coca-Cola's Senior Vice President, Director of Global Marketing, addressed an international conference on 'Global Beverage Marketing: Getting Ready for the 21st Century'. Coca-Cola is now perceived by many to be the archetype of a global marketing company. Similarly, in 1987 Procter & Gamble did not consider itself to be a global company. In 1992 it does.

Those five years mark a major shift in thinking towards global marketing. The gurus have established some common ground, if not true understanding. The biggest international companies claim to be, or to be going, global. Unfortunately the word has come to mean different things to different CEOs.

The loosest approach is to say that there are only three regions that matter: North America, Europe and the Pacific Basin. Any company well grounded in at least two of those can be considered 'global'. The strictest definition is close to Levitt's original: an organization that views the world as a single market place for which there is a single marketing plan, with uniform programmes, and a single coordinated production and distribution system. Products are made wherever the customer delivered costs are minimized. Everything is standardized; decisions are centralized. Few companies meet that definition, but many lean towards it. Ford, for example, aims to meet Japanese competition by using its worldwide geographic base to produce 'world cars'.

## 2.  MULTI-LOCAL V GLOBAL

Some see multi-local and global as ends of a spectrum. Every market can be treated as completely the same, or as completely different. To find a rational middle position, one can plot the economies of scale against the benefits of bespoke attention to each market. The benefits of scale are not just in engineering and production. R&D in pharmaceuticals, for example, needs the widest possible sales outlet and the least possible internal duplication. News media, from electronic to print, are increasingly sharing their collection, collation and editing costs. Partly or fully standardized material is beamed for local printing or broadcasting. Rupert Murdoch and Conrad Black clash worldwide. The BBC now competes with CNN. The multi-local to global spectrum does not tell the full story. Globalizing is not the same as standardizing. A global marketer treats the world as one marketplace and one source of supply. National boundaries are just a form of segmentation; the global company can segment in many other ways. So long as the advantages of variety outweigh the costs of production and reaching the consumer, the global marketer can compete in as many niches as it chooses. With the automation of more and more intelligence into production lines, it is possible to match consumer choice quite precisely with output.

Benefits of scale in marketing programmes are more difficult to quantify. When Pepsi recruited Michael Jackson for a global advertisement, the impact was huge but so was the cost. International advertising agencies are keen to peddle the global, or at least regional, line; two weeks making one Euro-commercial in twelve country formats costs less than twelve different commercials at a week each. International agencies ride these trends at the expense of their local counterparts.

Even if economies of scale (and the dis-economies) could be quantified, how will the benefits of local versus global be measured? After all, world scale sells airlines, computers and software. The people who use airlines travel; they like to know that service will also exist where they land. International brands can carry more status and therefore price. International branded whiskies, rum and vodka have been growing in Europe when local spirits have been falling. The 'imported' label still adds value in the USA.

One conclusion is that, measurable or not, some products fit the global dimension better than others. New technology is new to everyone and therefore has global marketing propensity.

Food and drink, however, are traditional products imbued with local cultural associations. How true is this? Are not Big Mac and Coke universal food and drink brands? Protagonists of global marketing argue that young people are less culturally rooted; what may be meat and drink to their elders are acceptable facets of American culture to them. Most examples also have counter-arguments and rationalizations made to fit. This path ends with the revelation that some products globalize better than others; particularly, the more premium brands, relative to their immediate competition, are likely to internationalize more readily. Otherwise, the difference between the products that do and the products that don't becomes clear only after the event!

## 2. DO GLOBAL BRANDS WORK?

If you wish to abandon that ship in haste, try the lifeboat called 'The Shrinking World'. Airports are clogged; planes queue to leave and land; Japan could not handle its own population if everyone came home at the same time. Even if everyone is not travelling, our TV screens are filled with foreign images. Brands offer consistency, right? Then surely our confidence will be shaken if we find different packaging, pricing, and positioning for our favourite brands as we travel from place to place? Most premium brands have globe-trotting consumers and are more dependent on their psycho-social benefits ('image' to you and me). For them, inconsistencies are more likely to be damaging.

On the other hand, one wonders how much the brain discounts differences in a place where it expects to finds differences. A Scot knows Germany is foreign before he gets there. If his favourite breakfast cereal is in a different package in German supermarkets, is he less likely to buy it when he gets home? Over the course of ten years, Absolut vodka grew from launch to a dominant position amongst premium vodkas in the USA. At the same time, it was sold at a discount in Canada. There was a three thousand mile, well trodden border between Absolut priced at 60 per cent more than Smirnoff on the American side and 20 per cent less on the Canadian (and in Canada, the brand did not sell). If brand consistency mattered, it did not show.

Economies of scale apart, why do CEOs aspire to be global? Evidence for profitability is conflicting, yet globalization is the trend. If competition goes global, the pressure to do so is reciprocally increased. If he hurts you in one place, you need to be able to hurt him somewhere else. At the same time those who over-reach themselves lose a great deal of money and, worse, impetus. The Midland Bank did itself no favours in trying to be too ambitious. Acquisitions are a particular hazard. In this case, one in the USA. Laura Ashley grew organically but also had to retrench with a new investor and new management. Even if going global is directionally right, how do we know where to stop?

Evolution is in one direction. Those who successfully achieve increased globality do not go back. How far should a company move towards a global objective in the short term? And why are we agonizing anyway? Other multinational functions, finance first, then accounting and R&D were globalized long ago.

But these functions interact minimally with consumers, and inter-country variation is not a factor in designing systems. Human resource practices, however, are indeed affected by cultural diversity and share the problems of marketing to differing value systems; yet in making comparison with these internal functions, are we being too introspective? Surely we should determine consumer needs through research? As a multi-national sees consumer needs converging around the world, should it not globalize?

The theory is sound, but in reality multi-nationals do not work that way. The increasing divergence of peoples in Yugoslavia, the old USSR, India and elsewhere around the world, makes a consumer driven demand for global standards incredible. Large marketing organizations are rightly driven by the future consumer's needs, which are unresearchable, not their needs of today.

The central driver towards globalization is the need to justify central overheads. This is not quite as cynical as it may sound. If all the business units were wholly oriented towards their own markets and heedless of the wider world, how would central management add value to the business? It would simply be an unnecessary cost, and the group would be better broken up and sold off; no wonder CEOs are keen to proclaim global tendencies. In fact, the central function adds value not only through cross-fertilizing best practices from one unit to another, but through the growth of corporate learning in the process. Idealists believe that such cross-fertilisation can be achieved by putting managers together so that they can recognize good solutions from each other's areas. No chance, they will see differences. Achieving the benefits from commonality needs central leadership.

Global marketing barely rates a chapter in most marketing textbooks because globalization has far more to do with organizational behaviour, human resource management and information systems than marketing functions. The core of an international airline is not the planes or the facilities or the engineering or the brand image, but the information systems and the knowledge the staff possess. Yet a global marketing organization can achieve results. Global learning allowed Procter & Gamble to launch its two in one shampoo/conditioner as Pert Plus in the USA and then under the Vidal Sassoon brand name (and called Wash 'N' Go in the UK and some other markets) in about 40 countries in the four years 1987-91. To do this, the company researched the key markets in parallel rather than sequentially as had been the norm. Then they used that learning to improve the original back in the USA. It is now a global brand.

Unilever took more than ten years to introduce Timotei, a similar product, to the same number of markets. What was the difference? Unilever had a more multi-local structure. Each general manager had his own turf and called his own shots. P&G and Unilever had matrix organizations, as every multi-brand multi-national does in one way or another, but in Unilever the country managers were the key decision makers. The difference was that Procter & Gamble had evolved towards a structure under which country managers share knowledge, turf and decision making to a greater extent. In Unilever at that time, the country managers were still barons.

This introspective concentration on managerial responsibilities is not misplaced. Until an organization can reconcile the roles of country, brand and top management, global marketing is impossible. Each company's solution may be different; the only common factor is that they must solve the problems.

The significance of electronic information systems for global marketing is not yet widely understood. It will be, probably the hard way. Global marketing, to be successful, requires shared decision-making which in turn demands improved communications and information; in other words, global learning.

## 3.  GLOBAL MARKETING ORGANIZATION

Within the marketing mix some elements are more standard than others. On a global to local scale a typical rank order is as follows:

*Variability of Marketing Mix Elements*

*Most standard*          – Brand name
                             Product
                             Packaging
                             Positioning
                             Advertising strategy
                             Price relative to key competitors
                             Advertising execution
                             Absolute pricing
                             Promotions
                             Customer service
*Most local/variable* – Personal selling

The marketer uses these levers in the best way possible. Efficiencies come from consumer segmentation. Historically segmentation has been by national boundaries. Now new segmentation choices are open.

In any particular company, the extent of standardization across national boundaries will vary, perhaps even from brand to brand. What is certain is that any form of global marketing requires leadership. In a single brand, worldwide business, leadership is supplied by the line managers. Multi-brand companies need some form of multi-dimensional structure, even though the 'matrix' as a term is out of fashion. Someone, somewhere, should be in charge of each brand if there is to be any coherence. Responsibilities have to be shared, or turf divided, between global, regional and national management. The most highly globalized companies need only a global marketing department and local sales companies. The most multi-local companies need a global brand coordinator with very limited powers. In between, pity the marketing manager in a country with both regional and global brand managers making demands in addition to the local hierarchy.

The costs and the confusion of excessive marketing bureaucracy can damage the health of brands. Most companies keep the levels to a maximum of two either by dropping the national level (rare) or sharing regional responsibilities on a 'lead country' basis. Under this system, each country assumes responsibility for one brand in that region (the EC for example) and accepts the leadership of colleagues for the other brands. The lead country then determines the standard solutions for the region, leaving the other elements of the marketing mix to be developed locally. The lead country also negotiates best regional solutions with the global brand manager. An alternative solution is for each country to deal with the global brand manager through regional specialists within a central global marketing department. In both cases, the regional bureaucracy can be kept to a minimum.

Almost any such solution seems confused to an outsider since it requires reconciling the unreconcilable: the decision-making autonomy of each level of the hierarchy. The corporate culture, not the structure, determines whether sharing is compatible with individual manager motivation. Structure is more visible than culture, yet it is corporate culture that determines whether any global marketing formula will work. If it encourages partnership and sharing, it will survive the problems of language and ethnic differences. So too will strong autocratic leadership, though it remains to be seen how long such an approach can deal with the subtleties and varieties of the world's marketplace.

Conversely, there are plenty of opportunities for global marketing organizations to fall apart. Why share information when to do so weakens one's position? Why do anything which does not maximize the profit of one's own unit? Internal transfer prices from one division to another are a classic area for dispute; so is the responsibility for the investment portion of the marketing spend, i.e. that part which will not earn its keep in the current financial period.

Strong international information systems and shared knowledge bases are symptoms of an organization that has already largely solved the corporate culture problem. To get there, country and brand managers' objectives, appraisals and accounting systems may have to be re-aligned to encourage cooperation rather than competition. Not all CEOs accept that. Many believe that the best results will come from a healthy competition between top managers or between their business units. To a very limited extent that is true: but in general, cooperation is more important. (See Compete or Cooperate?)

The purpose of management information is motivation and action. Who cares if the numbers are right if they prompt the right responses? The concerns with detail and independent accuracy so important for financial accounting may be less helpful for international managers needing to find shared directions. Central management can seem as if it is sending down tablets of printout from the burning computer to Moses in marketing. Many an international manager has been struck down by laser printer. Keep taking the tablets and you may be all right, but it is more likely that their weight will drag you down. Global companies need fast and light information, especially consumer information, that can promote effective marketing action on a wider scale than ever before.

The attention in this section has been on fmcg. In some ways the opportunities and benefits of globalization are stronger for services, notably financial services, and capital goods. But the principles remain the same: culture, information and shared learning are the keys.

If you can persuade:

1. Your group chief executive that internal cooperation is a better idea than arms length competition
2. The provision of figures that encourage it, e.g. double counting the profit so that both the country and the brand managers get the benefit of each others' good works
3. Your human resource department to have an incentive scheme that recognizes wider interests than just the parochial
4. Your information systems people to provide databases accessible by all

then global learning can begin. Global marketing will follow closely behind.

- **MEMO TO FILE**

*Subject:* GLOBAL MARKETING

- Rightly or wrongly, large international companies are going global. If your competition is likely to do it successfully, then do it first. But do not take too many steps at a time.
- Economies of scale may be a driving force, possibly marketing factors. Quantify them both. More likely, going global is a competitive strategy, not driven by economics. In the world poker game, globalization is upping the ante. The stakes are higher, the game is faster.
- Global does not necessarily mean universally standard. Segmentation and niche marketing may be more cost-effective within a global plan than using traditional national boundaries. Research markets in parallel, if your company is playing the global game, not in sequence.
- An international business adds value by cross-fertilizing successes from place to place, more likely at the strategic level, e.g. positioning of the marketing mix, than at the executional level, e.g. promotions.
- Forget structure, planning, analysis and bureaucracy. Global marketing requires an internal culture and information systems that foster shared corporate learning.

# 8.  The Genus 'guru'

**ISSUE:**

1.  Assessing what types of marketing people you have – are they doers, teachers or administrators?

Every marketing organization is made up of teachers, doers and administrators. If the numbers are well balanced and each is in the right place, lucky you. The importance of the teaching role for line management will not be news to anyone. Yet a discreet survey of your juniors may reveal that the roles are not distributed as they should be.

The Indian word for 'teacher' conjures up an image of an emaciated, ascetic mystic at one with the rhythms of the world, or maybe the next one. A Guru can impress students by standing on one leg. He does not need to move his position or his opinions. His advice is obscure but impressive. Fifty per cent of the time he is right; the rest you do not understand. Maybe he is surreptitiously spinning a coin.

A Guru has absolutely no urge to do anything. This is quite distinct from his more ambitious students. They can do everything, or so they think. One day they too may become Gurus but at this stage of life their behaviour identifies them as 'Kangurus'.

Kangurus are enthusiastic. They may confuse achievement with activity, be wrong 80 per cent of the time and yet be hugely successful. Small failures bring large successes. Sheer energy leads one jump to another, until gold is struck.

The two-legged Kanguru is easily distinguished from the 'Kan'tguru' encountered in important positions in large organizations. He or she has no legs and therefore limited movement. How they reproduce themselves so widely is something of a mystery. Kan'tgurus never make a wrong decisions because they never make decisions. They get about on the backs of the Kangurus whom they cultivate assiduously. Kan'tgurus can see both sides of any issue. They are considered 'sound'. The more astute reach high office.

The match between teachers, doers and administrators and the genus 'Guru' is not exact but it should give pause for thought before handing out the prizes on Speech Day. The happy smiling faces the Chief Guru sees looking down from his pedestal is a view quite different from that of those closer to the clay.

Are line managers teaching their team enthusiastically to apply what they themselves have learnt? Line managers should be progressing successfully from Kanguru to Guru. The junior members of the team can distinguish the Kan'tgurus from the Kangurus. Can you?

- **MEMO TO FILE**

*Subject:* THE GENUS 'GURU'

- Use professional research to find out what the team thinks of their own, and their seniors', efforts and contribution.
- You need a few Gurus and Kan'tgurus but only a few. How can you maximize the productivity of the Kangurus?

# 9. Hubris and the trade press

**ISSUE:**

1. Competitors read the trade press more carefully than customers. Marketing the trade press messages is a long way from boasting. What is the desired effect?

Some marketers are born humble; others have humility thrust upon them. Most marketers manage enough charm to keep it well concealed, but success tends to breed that cockiness which is more elegantly called hubris.

Hubris is the feeling of satisfaction that one knows at least some of the answers. The ancient Greeks believed that hubris was followed by nemesis. Pleasure in finding one's name on the Honours List, for example, (particularly on Harold Wilson's Honours List), was bound to be followed by falling into some metaphorical cowpat. Marketers are especially vulnerable to hubris because of the risk of believing their own publicity.

Hubris in business can be expensive. A famous example was the appearance of Gerald Ratner at the Albert Hall in 1991. An unguarded speech, which had previously amused many smaller groups with its candour, hit the front pages of the tabloids. He used a word tailored to their headlines: crap. It only applied to one item in his extensive range of jewellery products, but one was enough. Lack of respect for one's own products and customers is rank bad marketing.

We cannot disentangle how much of the fall of Ratner was due to the four letter word and how much to over-extending the business, high gearing, recession or the general decline in the jewellery market. But after the Albert Hall, the value of the company fell 95 per cent. Ratner's slogan, 'the lowest prices in town', applied to the shares as they fell to 21.5p from 389p. Within three months, Gerald Ratner was ousted from the chairmanship.

Hubris rarely meets nemesis so spectacularly. More routine but less dramatic examples can be found in the columns of the trade press, where product marketers hype their seasonal offerings. The motivation for the hubris is clear and it is good: we need the maximum publicity for our brand and its promotion. We must be positive and confident. Customers should know we have found the formula that will give retailers riches beyond the dreams of the Sainsburys. The trade press is a cost efficient way to reach customers. Editors need material to fill the gaps between the advertisements, so let's tell them what we're doing so successfully. Everyone is happy.

Happiest of all will be the competitors who will read all about it and react accordingly. Ultimately all communications to customers get back to the competition but exposing one's plans in the trade press ensures that such information is timely and reliable. But surely marketers are not so gullible? Surely the trade press is being craftily manipulated to provide disinformation for the competition? Aren't messages being planted to confuse competitors?

Maybe, but then again, maybe not. Sophisticated marketers have long since brought trade PR under full control, but elsewhere the column inches of vainglorious messages raise real doubts about their intended purpose. The availability of trade press for competitive signalling is important, but the opportunity for disinformation is limited. Few of us are clever enough to mislead competitors without disinforming customers at the same time.

Brand managers see public conferences and trade media as channels for the good news about their brands. So they are. The channels need to be managed, though, from the outside in. The desired effects on customers and competition need to be determined *before* the messages are designed. When there are messages for competition but not customers, or vice versa, then find another medium.

The trade press is the Cinderella of the marketing mix. Agencies and companies alike are disdainful. Consumer advertising and the national press are perceived as important; television still more so. Only top management can handle the cameras. Of course that is not vanity, it is just making the best use of experience! In the end senior management has so many commitments that trade press is left to Johnny who came lately. It will be good experience for him, say his superiors. That Johnny sees his name in print is probably the best part of the process; it may make a welcome morale booster after his plan has been ripped apart for the third time. Well, good for Johnny. Less good may be the injudicious use of space. Simple puffery for his brand may be doing more harm than good.

Manipulating customers' reading matter is a valuable marketing lever. A trade marketing department, if you have one, can increase the professionalism of customer communication. Marketing messages themselves need to be marketed; the competition will be reading the trade media over your shoulder. Watch out for hubris. Just because you are paranoid doesn't mean nemesis isn't out to get you.

- **MEMO TO FILE**

*Subject:* HUBRIS AND THE TRADE PRESS

- Take the trade press seriously.
- Resist hubris.
- Do you have full control of your competitive messages?
- Do you actively manage the messages to achieve the required effect?

# 10. Information systems survival kit

**ISSUES:**

1. Marketing is now faced with data-glut.
2. Need for clear process for maximizing benefit.
3. Crisis or complacency.
4. Developing machine analysis.
5. Practical steps to stay ahead of competition.
6. Systems assurance.
7. Releasing management for the marketplace and innovation.

## 1. DATA-GLUT

Once upon a time, marketers could expect intermittent sales figures, Neilsen and other market research data, records of their expenditure and precious little else. Today, their offices have information pouring out of every orifice. Hundreds of public databases, syndicated on-line market research, consumer panels and databases, customer records and internal databases add up to glut. Managers may be stimulated, or swamped, by the new excess. Can they benefit or will the next byte be fatal?

Both computer neurotics and computer literates need a survival kit. Whatever their situation now, an information avalanche is just waiting to fall. Maybe it is already falling. The prime cause of this is the electronic till.

At the end of every marketing chain is a consumer's cash or cheque or plastic card. All those trillions of transactions were never recorded till, no pun intended, now. Today, every purchase, every pairing of consumer and brand, can be held on a database if someone thinks it is worthwhile. What was bought, the date, time, price, where it was in the store and whether it was on promotion; and on the consumer's side, who you are, where you live, how much you spend, details of your family and your credit rating can all be recorded. Concerns for privacy will increase legal restraints on use, but the information is there.

Information systems professionals came late to an understanding of the needs of marketing. Perhaps the complexity of marketing requires more sophistication and hardware capacity than other functions; payroll, accounts, distribution, production, assets recording are all more amenable to numeric processing. Such transaction based systems had clear payoffs which were easy to measure. The importance of information to marketing is recognized, but the provision is lacking. What has been available has been in job lots. Internal sales statistics are geared to differing territories. Forecasts cannot be reconciled. Research suppliers each do their own thing. Nothing fits together.

Information specialists have long distinguished between data, the raw material, and information, data transformed into a usable format. The armed forces go one step further and call actionable information 'intelligence'. Those who think 'military intelligence' a contradiction in terms may be equally amused by 'marketing intelligence'.

## 2. NEED FOR A CLEAR PROCESS

In the commercial world, intelligence refers specifically to information about competitors but the wider sense is used here to indicate all information pre-processed for the user to eliminate dross and highlight possible action. The first component of an informations systems survival kit is a clear model of how to reduce the data glut to the stuff decisions are made of. The model here is:

Content            Process

Data
 ↓          Shaping and structuring
Information
 ↓          Analysis pre-processing
Intelligence
 ↓          Experience, creativity,
            intuition, teamwork
Decision

*Figure 5    From data to decision*

This is an idealized model. In practice decisions are made before any data is in, before it is processed. Information is used to support whatever it is one wants to do. The model assumes that, if one goes to the trouble and costs of collecting data, one should make the best of it. A rash assumption!

Designing the way a manager will see information sets, to some extent, the way it will be used. Either intentionally, or just through unconscious assumption, the layout of a page or screen formats the order in which the mind will assimilate what is presented and the direction in which it leads. More than that, the way information is presented influences not only the decisions reached, but the way we go about our jobs. To a large extent, we react to what we see and hear.

Few companies recognize that the way their computers shape and structure data for their managers also shapes the decisions that will ultimately be made. Incremental changes to systems refine what is already there but will not cope with today's nuclear explosion of information. Competition through the next generation will be substantially determined by the skill with which companies harness and use the data available.

The second component of the survival kit is to see the future and work back. A shared vision of how decision-making could be ideally served by information systems is made all the more necessary now that so much is possible. Only once that vision is agreed can one can get back to the pragmatic aspects of what to do next. This is emphatically *not* a call to design huge new systems starting on blank paper. Such grandiose schemes are almost invariably disastrous. Developing incrementally, step by step, has been good practice but systems cannot change direction as easily as people. New systems last for years. The direction has to be established.

The third component of the kit is a recognition that computers can be harnessed to do more of the 'grunt' analysis for managers, releasing them for creative and motivational tasks.

Fourth and finally comes information assurance. Marketing will become reliant on their machines. Systems failures may be a mild irritation today but they will be catastrophic tomorrow. What are the practical steps to robust systems?

## 3.   CRISIS OR COMPLACENCY?

To suggest that marketers are moving from data famine to glut may over-dramatize the situation, but those who fail to see both the opportunity and the competitive threat will reach a crisis.

Most companies and research specialists supply good information to their marketers, who are happy with what they receive. The cycle of planning, implementation, measurement and control proceeds with the regularity of the seasons. Performance measures have long been programmed and their continuity provides the bedrock of comparison.

Does that sound like complacency? Are we too comfortable with the present information and familiar presentation?

In reality, marketing information today lies somewhere between the extremes of crisis and complacency. Users may grumble, but they have themselves become programmed by the information they receive. We all adjust to routine no matter how outrageous that routine may be. In early 1992, UK newspapers were incensed by a man who, for 50 years, had locked his wife in the coal shed every time he went out. The wife could not understand what everyone else was fussing about; to her, this behaviour was perfectly normal.

The arrival of ubiquitous electronic data gathering is changing and will do more to change the practice of marketing than any other development. Why? It now takes the manager all available time just to pinpoint where the variances lie and what caused them. The machine should do that. The marketer should, when not in the marketplace and working with colleagues, be analysing the likely outcomes from alternative courses of action. When the machine is asked 'What if . . .', its answer should be matched against management intuition to strengthen decisions.

Whatever analysis can be routinized can be mechanized.

## 4. DEVELOPING MACHINE ANALYSIS

Some see analysis as the marketer's main function today. Developments from media buying, micro-economics, modelling consumer responses, decision-making and producing integrated, consistent plans are all logical functions requiring careful dissection of the evidence available. These are important but largely mechanical tools.

Analysis, in marketing, should find the unexpected and track the differences down to their source. This is satisfying work for those who enjoy holding magnifying glasses over computer printout, but it is by no means heroic. Tracking the planning cycle illustrates some areas of analysis today compared with tomorrow.

### Today

A finished plan will set out the new year's sales volumes, market share and, one hopes, profits. The key performance indicators will have been broken down month by month, product by product and sales unit by sales unit. A sales unit may be territorial, by customer group, by key account, or by several of these. The brand's expected awareness and the shift of attitudes in response to the advertising and PR may also have been predicted. Distribution (i.e. how many retailers carry the brand) has various measures. The manager may have set some ambitious targets for sales in order to gain new accounts, the merchandisers may have to come up with more facings and displays, and other departments will need to ensure the customer is never out of stock. Not everyone can always meet these targets, and one of the arts of planning is to get your excuses in first.

However it is done, the planning process sets out a set of performance benchmarks for the year to come which can be, but often are not, broken down to the same level of detail as weekly or monthly performance reports.

As the year progresses, actual results are matched up with plan and previous year figures. Variances are explained by breaking the figures down to the next level of detail, or the next again, until the source of the discrepancy can be identified. It is at this point that many information systems fail. Forecasts prepared by other departments may not match those from marketing; lower levels of detail may not be available; comparatives may relate to the previous organization structure. Eventually someone will produce that great inanity: 'the plan was wrong'. Of course 'the plan was wrong'. All plans are. They would not be much use if they were right; no one would learn anything.

A few steps down the analysis trail reveals what managers first look for. Programs can highlight significant differences and delve deeper to find numeric 'causes'. These are not true causes; they do not explain what brought the difference about. All they do is to show the numeric origins of the difference; they pinpoint the lowest level of detail. Why are sales down? 'Most of the decline is in Durham', might be the best available answer. Don't knock it. Few managers do better on their own.

However, the analysis and figure checking have absorbed most of the free energy. Forget fixing the problem for the future; the manager is only too pleased to have located it.

### Tomorrow

Contrast that scenario with the future: when the computer itself has mastered all the number crunching and become an 'expert system'. It has its tentacles into every database available and knows how to reconcile the inconsistencies. Every day it greets its manager with a brief summary of the most important facts resulting from its overnight analysis.

Writing the annual plan is no longer a number crunching chore for the manager. He or she can ask 'what if' questions and have the machine figure out the consequences. For each decision option, the computer can calculate sales, market share and profit. The machine will take competitive response into account. If the computer does not like the option, it will explain why. The manager can determine the preferred solution.

The marketing plan is reconciled with other departments' plans. Anomalies are highlighted for discussion between colleagues. Once everyone has agreed, the machine breaks the figures down to the lowest levels to provide forecasts for logistics (purchasing, production and distribution) and detail for comparison with actual results once the year in question begins.

This is no polemic for planning. Many companies get along just fine without it. They leave decisions to be made just in time by those on the spot. On the other hand those companies that do project a whole mass of numbers, at whatever level, ought to take the benefit that the computer can bring.

Some may find this future frightening. Others will be only to glad to dispense with numeric chores. The marketing department of today is likely to be disfigured, so to speak, by piles of printout and the oaths of juniors pecking at keyboards. Those who went to school before PCs were handed out to primary schools (1980) may never recover from computer neurosis. The electronic arms of technology are being wrapped around us, and terms like 'user-friendly' do not help. Who wants a user-friendly octopus?

Many people have been sold computer dreams before and been seared by the reality. False information system dawns are not uncommon and today the vision of turning analysis over to the machine may still seem like just that: a vision. The transition will happen, but more slowly than computer romanticists may claim. At the beginning of the 1980s, some savants were forecasting the decline of passive, or one-way, media (e.g.

newspapers, radio and television) in favour of interactive media. The consumer would insist on communicating with the communicators. By the turn of the century, it was said, print would be done for. Which century was that?

## 5. PRACTICAL STEPS TO STAY AHEAD

'Visions' are valuable components in planning. They do not have to be precise, have dates or pay bonuses. On the other hand they do need to be agreed, consistent and provide steady year to year direction. Visions may never happen but they enable progressive development.

In our survival kit, vision allows marketers to develop systems by working back from end decisions to the intelligence, the analysis, the information and ultimately the data needed to make them. That enables swathes of nice-to-know, but ultimately irrelevant, data to be eliminated from the system. Including everything is certain constipation. Beware the information junkie; however much is available, he still cries for more, to postpone the day of decision.

Another way to develop systems is to work back from the future to tomorrow to today. Expert marketing systems are some way off but experiments are proceeding and will increase. Creative advertising briefs have been successfully produced using expert systems. The first step is both possible and valuable today: exception reporting. Would you like your friendly PC to greet you in the morning with a list of the most important exceptions it distilled overnight while you slept? You can have that tomorrow if you tell your IS professionals what you consider 'important exceptions' to be.

Few managers can handle all the data and information they have today, still less the mega-bytes which are coming on stream. The first step is not to be intimidated by scale. Try imagining what information one would really want if the world market was just a village of a hundred people, if everything was on a human scale. To do that, forget the information you are used to having. What would you want to know about the customer, the brand, the consumer and the competition? Never mind the nice-to-know, what information really affects your decisions?

Such consideration is a step towards handling the richness of electronic information becoming available. The great need is to reduce volume and complexity of information availability to human scale.

Surviving the information explosion is critical to surviving competition. Competitors will be making good use of technology even if you do not. Time has to be made for a ruthless study of future needs. A plan for information systems development needs to be agreed with the relevant specialists however long it takes or much it costs. Two years or ten years is negotiable. Deliberate development should not be.

The long-term ambition should be to harness the power of computing to provide a leap forward in analytic capability. 'What if' modelling and exception reporting are now possible. As soon as the computer is programmed to identify the exceptional, the path to expert systems has begun. Marketing information has been supply driven for too long; marketers have had to put up with whatever they could get. Now for the first time marketing principles can themselves be applied to the provision of marketing information. It is time for marketing information to be demand driven.

The other practical steps are:

- *Forget the whole idea of 'integrated systems'.* Data needs to be integrated into shared databases to ensure accuracy, consistency and efficiency for multiple users. That is distinct from trying to integrate the systems that manipulate those data. Integrating systems is trying to complete a jigsaw puzzle with missing pieces which keep changing. Better let independent systems bring data in, manipulate them and take information out. Changing any one will not affect the others. Integrated data yes, systems no.
- *Equally daft is to match systems with organization structure.* Good organizations change several times faster than systems. Job-centred systems follow their managers from one structure to the next and withstand organizational change.
- *Information should be a commonwealth for everyone in the organization.* New information should be contributed to the

common pool to be shared by all. Confidential information will have to be partitioned, but how confidential is it? Who says it is confidential and why? More harm is done in large organizations by concealing information than by releasing it.

- *In designing job-centred systems, the opportunity exists to review job content.* In large fmcg marketing companies, the product manager's role has become so complex that it is being divided. Typically, trade or customer marketing roles are being created so that the product manager can concentrate on the consumer. The availability of better customer and promotional information can move the smaller marketing decisions from the centre to the field. Sales people are using mobile and home computers to access central data bases and make local decisions in place of national ones. Precision brings less waste and more profit.

- *As we saw earlier, information and the way it is provided directs the way any job is performed.* The training role of IS has been under-estimated. A new planning system, for example, needs to start, not from the way planning is done now, but from the way top management wants planning to be done. The modern democratic ethos is uncomfortable with systems being designed top down, yet that is the logic. Senior managers should determine job centred systems for their people, albeit with full user participation. To abdicate IS is to abdicate training.

- *Mechanizing analysis, job reviews, training and top-down specification are a cornucopia of nightmares for most marketers.* The idea that the machine is taking over the marketer's function will not promote cooperation. Successful implementation depends on busy people recognizing that they could gain more than they lose. Participation is important. Determining how the future should look, the shared vision, is critical to acceptance of the process.

- *Finally, this increase of information, programmed analysis and machine intelligence has also created a dependency.* Companies already exist where the only asset truly crucial to their business is the information system. Airlines are one example; credit cards are another. With the increased richness of market data, information systems will become critical to marketers in all sectors.

## 6. SYSTEMS ASSURANCE

This is not the place to review the conventional strictures about data and information management. Suffice it to note that the highest quality standards are needed. Back up, verification, controls, elimination of inconsistencies and dirty data are expensive. 'Core' information where these highest standards will be maintained should be distinguished from the peripheral areas where error or loss will merely irritate.

Do not expect marketing managers or sales people to key information into the system. They will hate it, get it wrong and blame those they believe responsible. Professionalism is needed in the handling and processing of data.

Information systems need to be safe and certain.

## 7. RELEASING MANAGEMENT FOR WHAT MATTERS

Not all marketers will share this vision of the opportunities brought by the information explosion. Top management may see technology as an aid whereas those more closely involved may see it as a threat. Or the reverse may be the case; enthusiasm by marketers unmatched by top management.

The pace of development will be dictated by competition. The technology is already here. Marketing success does not depend on analysis; it is a valuable contribution but it is not the key. The more important components are creativity, innovation and putting it all together, or synthesis. Marketing has far more to do with managing relationships between brand, consumers and customers, than with numeric analysis.

Information systems have to be survived before they can be harnessed to realize that future; a future which allows marketers to leave the paperwork behind and get back to the marketplace.

- **MEMO TO FILE**

*Subject:* INFORMATION SYSTEMS SURVIVAL KIT

- Control your information explosion before it or the competition blows you away. Make time to step back and consider what information your marketers and sales people will really need in the future. Do your customers have better information than you do?
- *Do not* tailor information systems to suit organizational structure. Marketing structures change faster than any other. First clear out redundant processes, levels of management and systems. *Then* tailor IS to maximize the potential of each job starting with the greatest added value and then the next. If that forces a review of each job contribution, be glad.
- Marketing will become information system dependent. Implement professional standards to maintain high quality information with full security.
- Mechanize analysis. What is routine can be programmed. The more analysis the computer can do the more time will be available for well informed innovation and coordination. Marketers belong in the marketplace.

# 11.  Isaiah principle

**ISSUE:**

1. The single biggest factor obstructing good marketing teamwork is the idea that one's territory is so different that there is nothing to learn. Successful businesses recognize differences but profit from the similarities.

John Donne declared that no man is an I-land. He was plum wrong. All of us establish our own turf to some extent, some little plot that is forever ours. Chief executives are the worst. They did not get where they are today without marking out a few boundaries.

The independence of one's own turf is shown by its differences from the patch next door. The size of the territory is immaterial. A sales manager in Manchester thinks his area is totally different from that in Leeds. To the UK manager in London, both look much the same but his own country is totally different to France. To the global manager in Tokyo all Europeans are much of a muchness.

In marketing, these parochial perspectives become a nightmare when one wants to cross-fertilize success from one market to another. Multinationals today are solving the problems because they have to. Left to their own devices, country managers are the least accurate forecasters of which successes elsewhere can be repeated in the countries they are supposed to know best. Why? Because the ego-drive that took them to being country managers now obstructs vision.

There are a number of I words that contribute to the I problem: individual, independence, insecurity, income. If the guy is profit responsible then he has to call the shots, right? Maybe.

The way multinationals are solving the problem is to recognize that there is a higher I, the seeing eye. (OK, this is better on the radio.) Somehow managers have to be able to recognize the similarities without being blinded by the differences, because it is through exploiting the similarities that multinationals make their money. International marketing has to pay close attention to the diversity of cultures, the traps set by language, variations in economic development and spending power, family relationships. These and many other factors will radically change demand as one crosses boundaries and yet brands do travel as well as people.

The Isaiah Principle states that it is profitable to pay more attention to the higher eye that sees the similarities between markets than to the lower I which uses differences to reinforce self image and status.

● **MEMO TO FILE**

*Subject:* ISAIAH PRINCIPLE

● Develop management culture, attitudes and finally structure that reward vision as much as status.

● PS My brother's called Isaiah because one eye's 'igher than . . .

# J

## 12. Beyond the J Curve

**ISSUES:**

1. Unexplained upturns in plans should not be accepted.
2. Brands may be myths but marketing is not magic.
3. What substantiates changes in customer and/or consumer responses.

The scene is the boardroom. It is marketing plan presentation day. In a long list of signals which trigger sales of stock options (new corporate offices, awards for business success, record levels of Group CEO benefits) the marketing department's use of expensive slides, or computer graphics, rather than cheap overhead transparencies must feature high. This is such a day. The health fanatics in Human Resources have banned tobacco despite the proven benefits to the company's pension fund.

In professional tones worthy of an undertaker, the first presenter describes how sales, market share and profitability have been sliding steadily. The sympathy of the audience is won immediately. Predecessors (apt word) somehow avoided the issues. Here is someone with courage, candour and objectivity. Thirty screens later the audience is clear that things are bad, they are going to get worse before they get better, that investment is needed but that the upturn will bring rewards beyond their ken. (Ken being the Finance Director).

Here is the all purpose 'J curve', otherwise known as the 'hockey stick', for these occasions:

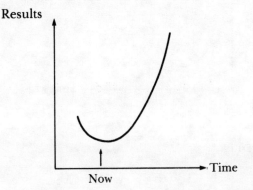

*Figure 6    The J Curve:1*

A well orchestrated presentation carries the audience towards what they want to believe: the happy ending. Emotional commitment will be strong. The advertising agency, sales management, market research all testify that they believe this plan. Key customers have been pre-sold. At last the right team is in place, the plan and the determination.

Apart from rank disbelief, what can one say?

The forecast could be true. Blind faith is a powerful force, especially when one has run out of other ideas. The J curve has particular attraction for those who do not expect to be around when the long term benefits are supposed to roll in. But it could be true because repositioning brands, advertising and much of the most important structural work takes time to show the gain. Maybe past investment really is about to pay off.

Maybe the business is cyclical: you can drop the J in figure 7 overleaf into the business cycle in figure 8 and it makes good sense. The change in results in figure 9, which incorporates the same J, calls for a dramatic explanation.

addresses the issue in the same terms the marketers used before they came up with their presentation, you will reach the same

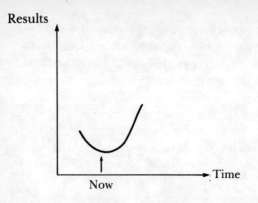

*Figure 7   Credible?*

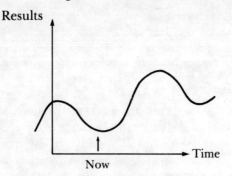

*Figure 8   In here it is*

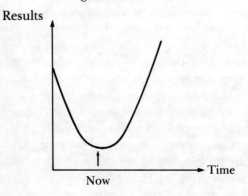

*Figure 9   In here it is not*

answer. You will find a forecast based on faith, not rationale. Stepping back to a longer focus may give make sense of the picture. Maybe a set of considerations are missing. It is tough looking for what is missing when you do not know what to look for. One candidate is the chosen market.

The fascination some have for market share is strange. Consumers do not buy markets or categories, they buy products and brands. "Markets" are groupings artificially brought together by managers predisposed by nursery training to tidy things into heaps. Take Lucozade, for example. Beechams sold ethical drugs, over the counter drugs (not unethical but not quite so superior) and Lucozade as a pick-me-up for convalescents. Faced by a galaxy of new formulations, boring old flavoured glucose and water was a pale and sick remedy for pale and sick people. Market share remained a healthy 100 per cent but sales did not look so good. Convalescence itself is outmoded; if you get tea and a biscuit after your operation you are doing well. Somebody somewhere in Beecham or its advertising agency changed the market, or the paradigm. Lucozade was now to be positioned as a healthy drink for the already healthy. As the drink for athletes to restore energy, what could be better? Daley Thompson personalized the brand's switch from wimp to Britain's decathalon hero. The investment was made; the J curve materialized.

Ask the consumer. Focus groups should not be used where you don't think you have the answer but who needs rules? Get a group going with a whole bunch of random thoughts about this particular market. See how they talk about brand usage and how consumption patterns are changing. How do other countries use the brand or its product equivalents? One way or another the neat box used to serve up the J curve in that presentation has to be torn apart so that real reasons for the upturn can be found.

● **MEMO TO FILE**


*Subject:* BEYOND THE J CURVE


● We all want to believe in happy endings but do not be carried along. If the reason for the upswing of the J curve cannot be identified, withhold investment.

# K

# 13.   Kotler – King of the textbooks

**ISSUE:**

1.   What books might one expect on marketers' shelves?

Marketing skills, like any other, are acquired by doing. After what seems an eternity in the education production line, the junior marketing manager wants action. Precisely the attitude the employer expects. Forget the textbooks. The advertising and marketing trade press provide, in digestible format, most of the written words any marketing manager needs to keep up to date.

Marketing is so context dependent that the specificity of the trade press is a positive help. Much of the competitive hype may not be credible but it is liberally doused with the salt of doubt and the vinegar of unwelcome gossip. Sample: 'Marketing Director Smith said the campaign was on course and would spend £10m this autumn. Those in the know put the figure under £5m.'

Nevertheless the pressures of day to day business and the ephemera of the trade press do not provide the mental anchor points for a career in marketing, and that means anyone in business. What are the definitive textbooks or even the passing good reads that should be found on a serious marketer's bookshelf?

- Philip Kotler's *Marketing Management. Analysis, planning, implementation and control* (Prentice Hall, 1991). This is the main MBA marketing text worldwide and has been for 25 years. Now in its 7th edition, its 756 pages contain all a product manager needs to know about marketing, as it is classically taught. Even those on full time learning struggle with it but as a reference work it is invaluable. Kotler brings order and discipline to every branch of marketing.

- Glen Urban's *'Advanced Marketing Strategy: phenomena, analysis and decisions'* (Prentice Hall, 1991). Perhaps the next step up for serious analysts.

- Hugh Davidson's *'Offensive Marketing'* (Penguin Books, 1987). Both the above are American. This is British but with a cosmopolitan tone. First published 1972 but extensively revised in 1987, it appeals to the pragmatic. As the name implies the accent is on keeping the initiative developing, from his key acronym POISE (Profitable Offensive Integrated Strategic and Effectively Executed). This is probably the marketing book to read next.

- Advertising has generated plenty of literature for and against. Those against have argued that it is either unethical, manipulative or ineffective. Or all three! Vance Packard with *'Hidden Persuaders'* (Penguin Books, 1981) was an early challenge. Plenty have entered the sport, on both sides, since. Marketing freedoms are under constant attack in developed countries. Serious marketers are expected to do their bit to defend legitimate interests both for themselves and consumers. Maintaining standards of practice are part of that defence. At the lowest they are enlightened self interest.

- Marketers are dedicated to understanding consumers in diverse cultures around the world. It is good to have a few representatives across this spectrum. Every new season has the new crop. One basic book for the world traveller's kit bag is *'Cultures and Organisations. Software of the Mind'* (McGraw Hill, 1991) by Geert Hofstede. This has tracked across 20 years of research the different country cultures as they show up in 100,000 employees of IBM. Factor analysis reveals how countries differ and confirms, to some extent, that stereotypes do work.

- Any book with 'mega' or 'wave' or 'beginning' or 'trend' or 'end' indicates the breadth of the reader's perspective? Of course it does. A current sample is Francis Fukuyama's *'The End of History and the Last Man'*. (Hamish Hamilton, 1992).

- Books by Michael Porter and other economists require no further comment from me.

- Al Ries and Jack Trout have written several readable and stimulating short books on marketing's cut and thrust. *'Positioning'*, *'Marketing Warfare'* and *'Bottom up Marketing'* are all published by McGraw-Hill.

- Winston Fletcher has also written some fun books from an advertising agency viewpoint. His *'Meetings, Meetings'* (Michael Joseph, 1983) now seems to be out of print. See if you can take my copy from whoever stole it from me.

- Chris Macrae has been deeply involved in applying mathematical models to brand launches and other marketing problems. His *'World Class Brands'* (Addison Wesley, 1991) balances the picture with some nice anecdotes and perspectives.

- *The Art of War* (or 'Strategy', translations vary) by Sun Tzu (various editions available), written over 2,000 years ago, is still every strategist's primer.

- Rosabeth Moss Kanter deals with change in organizations. *'When Giants Learn to Dance'* (Simon & Schuster, 1989) follows on from *The Changemasters*.

- There are various dictionaries of marketing terms. My favourite is by Michael Baker. (2nd edition, Macmillan 1990). He has also contributed an important textbook: *Marketing: An Introductory Text* (5th edition, Macmillan, 1991)

- Robert Townsend's *Up the Organisation* (Michael Joseph, 1970) may be old, but it is a classic. Instant sense. If you only have room for one book besides Kotler, this should be the one.

● **MEMO TO FILE**

*Subject:* MARKETING TEXTBOOKS

● Spend half an hour browsing in a business book shop. Whether you ever read what you then buy is secondary. You will have stepped back from the action long enough to re-think what marketing is all about.

# 14.   The educated Lunch

**ISSUE:**

1.  Get away from roles and rituals for a free format focus on improvement, or a free lunch.

Call your company's marketing director at 2.45 and her secretary says 'She's in a meeting'. Is she really in a meeting or is this a well-trained secretary? You and I think she is still at lunch. We, sitting virtuously back at our desks, are able to make and take calls. 'Still' at lunch?

Lunch is perhaps the most important part of a marketing director's day. What may seem to be R&R (rest and relaxation) is truly an escape from R&R (roles and rituals). Lunch is an opportunity to break formality and to float ideas. Lunch may be the one opportunity for genuine marketing she gets all day. Most marketing directors regret they have so little time to do any marketing.

Lunch is the opportunity to teach, to be educated and to be a little bit crazy, all important aspects of marketing. The educated lunch is not about making decisions.

First let us consider the rituals:

- *On arrival at office:* deal with mail and paperwork. Return phone calls. Anticipate what might be bugging the boss. Ask the sales people why sales are not higher.
- *Before lunch:* meetings.
- *After lunch:* meetings.
- *Last thing in the office:* sign mail. Return calls from those you missed in the morning. They have gone home. Do not answer the phone which rings as you walk out, because at that time of day it is never good news.
- *Evening:* read all the paper work that arrived whilst you were in meetings.

The majority of meetings come in one of three forms: someone is selling something to you, you are selling something to somebody else, or you are wondering why you are there at all when there are plenty of other good meetings you could be at. All these meetings are 'decision-oriented'. The decision may be to meet again (or not) or to appoint a sub-committee. Minutes may be kept or not but loose talk is not popular. When decisions are not enough, meetings become 'action oriented'.

Meetings need to be short and to the point. Large meetings are good for information, coordination and decision, small meetings are good for creativity and innovation. They all sustain, and are sustained by, rituals and roles. They develop regularities. They may be weekly or monthly, morning or afternoon; agendas become standardized. Those attending meetings fulfil the roles they have been given or assume. Meetings become predictable. Predictable becomes boring.

The educated lunch is a necessary release from all that. Marketing needs the balance of order and disorder. The body may be weighed down by Entrecote de Cardinal Richelieu and a bottle of Chambertin 1945 but if the mind liberates one great idea, it is all worthwhile (provided the resulting profits exceed the cost of the lunch). If a green salad and a bottle of Aqua Libra produces a better result for you, then go mad and order a second bottle.

The educated lunch must be distinguished from the working lunch. This abomination is a meeting continued over curling sandwiches. The slightly more upmarket variant provides salad, and allows you to drop mayonnaise on brand plans. There are other variants as well, romantic lunches, old boy/girl lunches, we-must-meet-again-but-now-we-have-was-it-a-good-idea? lunches, but none of these are designed to maximize the profit of the business. The educated lunch is serious in intent but light in tone. (There is also the educated breakfast or dinner for workaholics).

An educated lunch may take place with the agency, colleagues, competitors (often the best), customers, suppliers or anyone who can enjoy the escape but will also help you build your business. The first course may be a gossip or a moan about how business is terrible. The fish course is supposed to stimulate intellect. Some absolutely ridiculous notion should be challenged and defended. Then you are ready for the meat and potatoes of thinking and learning. A good lunch provides the intellectual protein and starch you need to fuel new ideas.

Meetings are for rituals, roles and vertical thinking. The educated lunch is a leveller; anyone present can propose or challenge an idea. We may not all be the same under the napkin but lateral, as distinct from horizontal, thinking is to be encouraged.

Finally, don't rush an educated lunch. You need the release.

- **MEMO TO FILE**

*Subject:* THE EDUCATED LUNCH

- Attach this essay to your next expense claim.

# 15. The evolution of Marketing

**ISSUES:**

1. Tell me again: what is 'marketing'?
2. Evolution from volume to cost to value.
3. Evolution from advertising to mass to micro.
4. Evolution from transaction economics to managing relationships.
5. Does marketing manipulate consumers? Economic necessity.
6. The choice of marketing systems.

## 1.  DEFINITIONS OF MARKETING

At its most general level 'marketing' is the presentation of a proposition in the way in which it is most likely to be accepted. Whether it is the packaging of a brand of cat food or the election manifesto of a political party, marketing is distinguished from other business activities by the way it takes the customer's point of view and looks back. But this is only the beginning: the customer's perspective may illuminate such weaknesses in the proposition that it needs to be totally changed. Marketing is not just advertising, promotions, packaging and other forms of presentation; it is the totality of the product.

Throughout this book 'customer' means the immediate

recipient of a sale. 'Consumers' are the end users. The ultimate customer is therefore the consumer. In the long run the consumer is king but to get there, the customer has to be satisfied first.

Evangelists market churches, charities market appeals, today even the police worry about marketing to the public. Whatever the category, marketing is the least painful way to achieve one's objectives.

Marketing has many associations, 'total quality' for example. Oriental martial arts share many of marketing's philosophies, including a highly developed sense of where the opponent is at.

Not-for-profit organizations are an important area of marketing where all sorts of non-monetary values get put on the table. But this book is concerned with the commercial arena; here marketing, quite straightforwardly, is about the making of money. 'Satisfying customer needs profitably' is a definition of sorts; crisp, yes, but deep, no.

There are as many definitions of marketing as there are marketing professors. In this book alone, it will be redefined several times. The reason for this is that we all have mental models which we use for solving real life problems. All models arise from our own experience, but some models only suit some problems. Soldiers see marketing as commercial warfare, economists as sets of equations, sociologists as groups making exchanges and statisticians see probabilities. Use any definition that applies your own mental model to the issue at hand. Marketing itself is the richer for the variety.

Marketing is complex but it is also dynamic. This chapter traces three ways of viewing the evolution of modern marketing:
1. There is a historical economic pattern which follows the development of production systems and the changing ways in which marketing adds most profit to the business. The trend has been from achieving volume, to reducing costs, to adding value.
2. Marketing has retained its close association with advertising since the turn of the century. As advertising was able to capitalize on mass media to increase size and breadth of appeal, marketing followed. Mass marketing keeps its place for some products but contracting economies have built direct marketing

methods using the new technology to focus resources far more closely on target markets. The trend from mass to micro-marketing is real but may overstate what is really an increasing choice between different marketing systems.

3. Marketing inherited strong traditions of economic thinking. The pressure to quantify, to measure the results of alternative programmes, will not change, but the perspective is changing. In general, focus is shifting from the single transaction, i.e. the sale, as the end point of the marketing process to the enduring relationship between consumer and brand. If the relationship is right, transactions will follow. Then there are all the relation-ships internationally between consumers, customers, distribu-tors, marketing agencies and the brand owner. Attention is now being focused on how best to manage these complex relation-ships in order to maximize short and long term profitability for the firm and the satisfaction for the consumer.

## 2. EVOLUTION 1: PRODUCTION EMPHASIS HAS SHIFTED FROM VOLUME TO COST TO VALUE

A Finance VP at Seagram once said, and it must have been second hand then, that there are only three ways to make money: sell more, make it for less and put the price up. It's not quite true, but it is an elegant essay on commercial evolution. Once the problem was to make enough of whatever it was. The world was short of everything; if you could make it, you stood a good chance of selling it. But man the manufacturer got better and better. Soon everyone was making everything. Competition became tough.

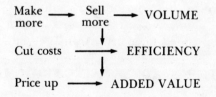

*Figure 10   The evolution of profits and marketing*

The market set lower selling prices. Profits went to those who could cut costs. Time and motion studies were born in the early years of the century. Black Model Ts rolled forth from assembly lines. Economies of scale encouraged growth and acquisition. Marginal costing allowed the big to grow bigger. As distribution improved and the world was perceived to shrink, production could be concentrated to serve the globe at lowest cost. Originally Ford erected plants to serve the needs of that country, then that region. Today each of its production units takes its place within a global production network: one production structure supplies one world marketplace. The process continues but a new wave has been building up behind the first two: value.

When everyone has one of everything, the only way out of the crowd is up. There comes some indefinable time when matching the neighbour's latest purchase is not enough: one has to go better. Raising the stakes in this particular social poker game requires others to play as well, and in boom years the neighbours play high. In a recession the cheapest may upstage but only for a while. It is quite permissable to scour Yellow Pages for a few pence off washing powder whilst spending an extra thousand pounds on car vanities. Happiness is a loaf of bread, a jug of wine and a few thou.

The evolution, therefore, is through production increases to cost cutting to value added, but not in a neat and orderly fashion. All three sources of profit continue to coexist, with the emphasis moved to value.

Marketing is managing that added value as well as identifying costs that can be cut without detriment to consumer benefit. It is about added sales. Marketing deals with all aspects of increasing profits, but with adding value most of all. As the returns from volume and cost reduction diminish, future profits will come from added value being translated into higher prices.

## 3. EVOLUTION 2: ADVERTISING FROM MASS TO MICRO

That the first model is expressed in accounting terms should be no surprise. It comes from an internal analysis of a business's profit and loss account. Marketers will identify more with the promotional model, for that is how they gain their experience.

The earlier chapter on advertising reviewed the way modern marketing was created by the media's need to sell space. The association between business and advertising has remained close. Some companies even have their advertising agencies write their marketing plans. Odd as this may seem today, there are advantages: objectivity, a deeper grounding of the advertising in the needs of the business, quality of thinking and saving overheads.

Through the 1960s marketing was seen as a largely promotional activity, adding glitz to whatever was put out by production. Marketers themselves, and the more advanced marketing companies, were well aware of the deeper, all embracing needs of consumer orientation, but for many companies such awareness was only skin deep. For sectors that developed late, such as financial services, marketing referred to advertising, promotions and prettying up whatever the consumer sees.

The 1970s presented marketers with a number of rude shocks. Oil prices created a crash and a recession. Inflation played havoc with media costs. Years of successful cost efficiency had made the mass media moguls greedy. Consumers began to broaden their use of media away from the main TV channels and top daily papers. At the same time, demand and reader/viewership were down and costs were up.

There was no watershed. Agency life was uncomfortable for a while but the highs and lows of agency life are endemic. Nevertheless, the mid 1970s marked the start of the development of direct marketing using new technology in order to achieve better accuracy in targeting.

There is nothing new about direct marketing as a concept: mail order, now rechristened 'catalogue marketing', had been around for generations. Telephone selling was available in the 1960s, albeit in primitive format. The most developed marketers were the direct mail companies themselves who could readily adapt their main medium. The difference lay in the database technology. Why do you think that one of the largest telephone selling (now called telemarketing) businesses in the world, is in Omaha, Nebraska? The large computer database technology used by this company was developed by people who learned those arts at the expense of the US government, at the HQ of Strategic Air Command located in that city.

The first area for development was lists. Names and addresses were bought from societies, other traders, book clubs or anything to which people belonged. The value of a list depended on how current it was and how accurate the names and addresses and the spending power of those included were. The consequence for the consumer was, of course, junk mail.

Computer technology has now made direct marketing interactive. The consumer can initiate matters by using the home computer to interrogate shopping directories (or, in the USA, using kiosks equipped with PC). Or the consumer can telephone a database and speak directly with the machine. Voice recognition systems in the UK are a little ahead of the USA at the time of writing; the preferred US system is for the consumer to respond to questions from the computer's voice synthesizer by pressing one of the touch tone keys on his or her telephone. In this way full orders can be placed. These computerized speaking machines have the advantage of being available 24 hours a day and handling peak traffic with fewer delays. Direct marketing reduces the number of stages in the distribution process and offers the convenience of in-home selection and sending gifts without visiting either stores or the Post Office.

In databases today, lists are still the key. Once logged in, however, they can begin to track purchases and identify those who purchase regularly or recently and the price brackets, quantities and types of products purchased. With that data the computer can predict more accurately than ever before those likely to buy in descending order of expected profit. With phone calls costing about £3 each and direct mail shots not much less, the costs and benefits can be tracked with some precision.

Telemarketing is reputed to have grown by 40 per cent per annum in the UK in the 1980s. Clearly this rate of increase will not continue but refinements to the databases and technology should maintain significant growth through the 1990s.

## 4. EVOLUTION 3: TRANSACTION ECONOMICS TO MANAGING RELATIONSHIPS

A between-wars advertisement for a whisky brand would include a fine picture of the bottle, a reason to buy ('Scotland's finest'), maybe a couple of glasses, and the price. They were trying to sell you a bottle of the stuff.

Today there may be no picture of the bottle, no overt reason to buy and certainly no price. They would like you to feel good about the brand, to believe that the lifestyle the brand seems to epitomize would mesh beneficially with your own lifestyle.

Japanese domestic advertising carries this concept much further. Westerners have to struggle to make any direct connection between the brand and the content of its Japanese TV commercial. However, the marketing intention is the same: if the consumer enjoys the sensations of the advertisement, then his relationship with the brand that paid for those sensations will be improved.

One practical consequence which concerns relationships has come from 'free call customer care lines' as Van den Berghs call them. In the USA, Pillsbury and a few other leading fast moving brand companies developed streamlined complaints procedures into powerful two-way consumer communications. Rather than have people write in, the pack carried an 800 number for consumers to call with any problems. It was easier and, important to the food industry, dangers could be picked up far more quickly.

It turned out that actual complaints amounted to 20 per cent or less of the calls. People phoned in for advice on using the product, to make suggestions, to say thank you, or just for a chat. Marketers recognized that rather than wait for cumbersome market research or customer information so consolidated it had lost all value, there was a rich bank of consumer data phoning itself in daily. Relationships could be assessed and nourished right on line.

The managing relationships model certainly has attractions: it fits better with concepts of brand equity and encouraging management to take a longer view of its responsibilities.

Industrial marketing, which is fundamentally about building enduring relationships and little about short-term transactions, can be reconciled with consumer marketing. The need to look through the customer's business to the consumer is rationalized by attending separately to managing customer relationships (sales and trade marketing) and the customer's relationships with the consumer (promotions and merchandising).

The shift of focus from transactions to relationships makes accountability more difficult to measure but also more important. There is always a risk that complexity becomes an excuse for waste.

## 5. DOES MARKETING MANIPULATE CONSUMERS?

The consumerist at this point may pick up a pen to record an old prejudice: marketing is manipulative. At the least, it causes consumers to buy what they do not need at artificially inflated prices which they cannot afford. Marketing may indeed provide 'added value', but for whom? There is a splendid ambiguity in the word 'value'. It can be the subject of endless academic theses, or pragmatically set at whatever someone will pay. *Why* we pay, the reasoning, the emotions, the trade-offs, may remain forever mysterious. The marketer is happy merely to note the sales outcomes of alternative marketing actions. The manufacturer may legitimately influence choice in favour and the Consumer's Association may legitimately recommend other uses for the consumer's money, but it is still the act of purchase that defines value.

A famous test case arose in washing powders. The UK duopoly of Procter & Gamble on the one hand and Unilever on the other hand was considered to be creating artificially high prices through marketing, and especially through advertising. The government ruled that each had to offer a cheaper alternative with minimal marketing cost. To forestall game playing, the brands had to be real, existing, well packaged and with comparable sales push. 'Square Deal Surf' was born and Tide was relaunched. Sales, after the initial ballyhoo, were poor. It was quietly accepted that the manufacturers, or more accurately, the consumers knew best.

At about the same time, subliminal advertising came under challenge. It was claimed that individual film frames showed advertising that passed too rapidly to be detected by the conscious brain but impacted the subconscious. In this way manufacturers could cause consumers to buy without awareness of the pressure to buy. The advertising world was surprised to hear that it did this. Having already taken the blame, some advertisers decided to give it a go. It did not work. Some governments then closed the stable door by banning it, and the episode was closed.

Then there was the accusation that sex was being used in advertising. Not the pictures of attractive young people that decorate or disfigure, according to your point of view, the promotion of cars in the 1960s and body care and ice cream today, but the actual word, disguised into advertisements for drink. A glass of Gilbey's Gin held three lumps of ice in which could be discerned, with a little imagination, the three naughty letters S, E, X. It may be a measure of the innocence of those days that this was supposed to send us scurrying to the off-licence. Certainly Gilbey's failed to take over the drinks market.

If real power to subvert people through marketing was available then it would indeed be dangerous, though one suspects that the public would wise up fast. The reality is that the power to change is very limited; marketing can prompt, remind, provide news, and give opportunities to purchase, and not much more. Advertising, as Andrew Ehrenberg so cogently puts it, is a very weak force which is why we need so much of it. Consumers respond to trends for reasons as incomprehensible to the marketer as anyone else. What the marketer is seeking to do is spot the trends and get just a little bit ahead of them. Marketing does not create waves; it aims to detect them and ride them and, maybe, blow up a few wavelets on top.

That marketing is so virtuous may strain credulity. Consumerists may not be receptive to the notion that marketing helps people solve their money problems. That notion works as follows: the western world is now riddled with pockets of affluence; our parents worked hard to make money believing it would bring comfort and they, or we, would be happy ever after. But things rarely work as planned; affluence turns out to be quite a burden. It's not one we want to give away, of course, but it is a new set of worries just the same.

Just when it all seems too difficult, enter the marketer. Your magazines, which have themselves been marketed to you, are full of ads and other helpful hints on how to spend money, spend time and money, and save time in order to spend more money. All of this is essential to the economy, which must grow so that we become still more affluent. The lack of marketing was the cause of the collapse of Eastern European governments: forget political philosophies, it was the absence of consumer-friendly brand managers that unglued the communists. No one was adding value in consumer terms. Now we see China attempting a more sophisticated reconciliation of totalitarian government with some freedom of markets. Is marketing going to save the world? Perhaps not. But it can help make it a slightly more pleasant place to live.

If the description of marketing as constant nudging, attention seeking, even intrusion, reminds you of a walk through an oriental souk, it should. Technology has changed but people haven't. Primitive circumstances needed primitive methods. Today's techniques will seem primitive to our successors but marketing will forever be what goes on in markets.

## 6. THE CHOICE OF MARKETING SYSTEMS

I have tried to show that marketing is ageless. It was not invented this century, as some believe, though modern methods are quite a transformation. Marketing concerns everyone trying to get other people to do what they want. What this century *did* invent is the marketing department. These specialize in the techniques, and in spending money. Are they necessary? Not strictly speaking, no, but they can produce far more profit than they cost.

This chapter concludes with a brief résumé of some of the modern marketing systems available.

## Industrial or business to business marketing

This system deals only with direct customers as distinct from the consumers who eventually use the product manufactured by the customer. For practical purposes (purists will quibble) this equates with the trade marketing leg of consumer marketing. In order to streamline the marketing roles in consumer-oriented companies, trade or customer marketing is increasingly being split away into separate departments, leaving brand or product managers to concentrate on the consumer.

## Network marketing

This is the use of personal contacts to build both sales and informal organizational structures and is also called multi-level marketing to reflect the importance of the structural relationships. Examples include Amway, Tupperware and, more recently, air and water home filtering systems. In contrast, *Networking*, or *'internal marketing'*, also refers to the needs of marketing managers to build personal 'selling' relationships within a large organization in order to get anything done.

## Direct marketing

This links with telemarketing and database marketing (using information systems to target customers and consumers, retain information and follow up). Some forms include the immediate take-up of a TV, radio or print advertisement. Cost benefits can be accurately assessed since the response to each individual advertisement can be measured. Direct marketing is also moving from its 'transactional' roots to the relationship approach provided by modern databases.

## Value marketing

This is a stage in the first evolutionary cycle. The philosophy here has moved away from the promotion of the sizzle back to the steak itself. In this view, the product is again the hero, margins are thinner and prices are lower. It is a partial, and therefore transient, model but it reflects the spirit of the 1990s.

*Integrated marketing* (should there be any other sort?)

This refers to the linking of direct marketing to general advertising and quite specifically to the sales force. Linking telephone selling and personal calling is not new. For example, the direct marketing effort will pull in the easier and less valuable business but will also throw up those accounts who want to see a sales person and whose business justifies it.

- **MEMO TO FILE**

*Subject:* THE EVOLUTION OF MARKETING

- Marketing is the art of using the customers' and consumers' points of view to achieve one's objectives with least time and resources. For a business that means maximizing short- and/or long-term profit, however these are defined.

- Apart from restructuring (acquisitions, disposals etc), there are only three ways to maximize profit, and these approximate to the evolution of business priorities:

  VOLUME → EFFICIENCY → ADDED VALUE

  Marketing contributes to all three but especially the last.

- The second evolutionary trend harnesses the power of databases to direct marketing allowing tighter focus of resources to targets and more accurate measurement.

- The third trend is to view marketing as the management of relationships: primarily that of brand personality with the consumer, but also those of intermediaries and the wider network of all those involved in the marketing process.

# 16. New it all along

**ISSUES:**

1. Marketing as 'organized rational innovation'. What does it take?
2. Change cultures and champions.
3. The agenda for innovation: the New Money Machine.
4. Should priorities set themselves?

## 1. INNOVATION IS CENTRAL TO MARKETING

'New, improved' is a tired old cliché which alerts consumer suspicions. Nevertheless our jaded palates demand both novelty and increasing quality. We like most of what we have but also crave a few changes. Changes spell marketing opportunity. Ken Simmonds, one of London Business School's luminaries, describes marketing as 'organized rational innovation' and calls that the eighth paradigm, or definition or model, of marketing. He analyses the previous seven to show how we all define marketing to suit our own training or experience. Economists see marketing as microeconomics, social scientists as interpersonal exchanges, architects as structures, militarists as commercial conflict or warfare. We can all rationalize the market-place to suit our own skills, but the perception of marketing as innovation lies deeper.

Whenever someone uncovers a new technique for making money, be sure you are not standing in the door. When the rush to imitate is done, that technique no longer makes money for new players. Marketers have to persuade their colleagues to innovate and then customers and consumers. The combination of more affluence, more choice of brands, media and retailers requires more innovation to stand out from the throng; it spoils consumers for choice. Today, innovation matters more but produces less. The challenge is on.

Brands require to be differentiated in order to command premium prices and achieve good levels of profit. This differentiation requires constant refreshment. Otherwise premiums disappear and brands become commodities. Domestic light bulbs were once heavily advertised brands. Remember Osram? Today few care, or could name, which bulbs they buy.

Innovation is more than creativity; it is the commercial realization of creativity. Deservedly or not, Britain is seen as creative but not innovative. Many analysts have crawled over the reasons for Britain's declining share of world trade, but their reasonings need not detain us here beyond the thought that the failure successfully to innovate and to market are one and the same. Innovation requires an enthusiasm for change and an enthusiasm for teamwork; creativity can be bought but innovation is down to you.

## 2. CHANGE CULTURES AND CHAMPIONS

The London 159 bus route was created in 1906 to run from North West London to deepest South. Generations of management fiddled with the route but 80 years later it was still attempting to traverse about 12 miles of traffic congestion from the western fringes of Hampstead to Thornton Heath. Only 159 bus drivers were able to find both extremities and not all of them. Waiting for a 159 gave a good impression of what eternity must be like. Following the reorganization of London Transport into smaller areas, decision-making moved closer to the garages.

In 1992 the route was divided into two: the 159 would go from Streatham into the centre and return, a new 139 service would go from Hampstead, overlap with the 159 to give extra buses where they were most needed and then return. The reluctance of the natives of Hampstead to visit Streatham was, in any case, matched by Streatham's disinterest in Hampstead. Splitting the route was a simple idea and an instant success. It was too radical for the previous regime which had no culture of change.

Some believe that any major alteration requires to be triggered by some crisis, real or imaginary. All change is pain; it needs a bigger pain to induce it. It is true that an organization set in its ways will need some major stimulus to adapt. On the other hand, modern companies are making change a way of life.

One can categorize change in any number of ways but by size it can split three ways:

1. Seismic shift following acquisition or a new CEO or a disaster or all three. The only seismic shift that concerns this book is changing a business to a market orientation if it does not have one already. That is more an issue of leadership than marketing. Talking culture change does not bring it about. On the other hand, a CEO who gets into the market-place, looks at marketing measures, asks market questions and pays by market-place results will rapidly induce a market orientation.

2. Major shift such as entry to a new product category, line of business, type of customer or country. Different organizations successfully adapt in different ways. One of the classics is the use of 'champions' pioneered by the 3M Corporation. These are senior managers with the muscle and know-how to crash the concept through the organizational barriers of inertia and negativism. The system only works when the manager develops a personal commitment and even an evangelical enthusiasm for the change. He or she needs to know the extent of the difficulties but understand how relationships can be managed to give the result. Sometimes the champion is the CEO but there is a limit to the number of such causes any one manager, or the organization as a whole, can handle. (The application of this principle to

radical new brand or product development is considered in 'Ugly Duckling'.)

3. Minor improvements are what the Japanese call *'Kai Zen'*. A well adapting company empowers all its employees to make constant small improvements to their areas of business. Total quality management is in vogue and shares with marketing the concept of seeing things from the customer and/or consumer viewpoint. The concept of empowerment is grand but implementation can be a nightmare. An 'improvement' by the sales person can be a step backwards for accounts.

If you have ever wondered what brand managers actually do, we have just got to the nub. Did you think they managed brands? Ah, well. Some elderly marketers have been known to disparage brand managers but they are quite wrong to do so. Of course a major brand is the life blood of the business; a CEO will ensure the health of that brand through close involvement and the brand manager will make a major contribution. The speciality, though, lies in bringing all those minor improvements made, in a large company, by very many people into harmony. That may not seem heroic but it is how Agincourt was won.

Marketing is 'organized rational innovation' and it is the brand manager who does the organizing and makes sure that the constant stream of innovations are rational. The culture of the organization needs to be developed to encourage continuous improvement.

## 3.   INTRODUCING THE NEW MONEY MACHINE

One of the evolutions of marketing reviewed in the last chapter was the historical priority for making money. In the beginning was volume: if you could make it, you could sell it. As production increased, the focus switched to costs: you had to make it for less. Quality was always an issue but as production skills improved again, the opportunities for cost reduction began to achieve diminishing returns. The post-60s developments looked increasingly for values that could be added to give the consumer more satisfaction than the utilitarian.

The New Money Machine applies this evolutionary principle to marketing planning. It is based on the one-armed bandit, not inappropriately some will think. Added values are the cherries. Even one will pay out and if you can get a whole line, the payout is handsome. Volumes, costs and added value need to line up before you make big money. Here's how it works:

1. Convene a meeting of top management in some oasis to review the organization's, and therefore their, future. The objective is to identify innovations, establish their credibility, costs and potential benefits. You may regard what follows as practical or just an agenda. The need is to free thinking from the shackles of convention.
2. Review the five year plan, brainstorm, let syndicates loose or do whatever you usually do to get the motivation and creative energies surging.
3. Recognize that new money will come from one of the three kinds of change outlined above. If it is seismic it is the CEO's job, major needs a champion and minor is for everyone with the brand manager, or equivalent, coordinating. Shifts are not necessarily positive; they can be expansion or contraction, plus or minus.
4. Major shifts can be territories, customers/channels of distribution, product categories, production and distribution techniques or facilities, competition entering, leaving or alliances. The game is to find who, with a little help from their colleagues, believes that significant new money can be found from that source. The believers are potential champions.
5. The appeal of one-armed bandits lies largely in the satisfaction of pulling that lever. The New Money Machine is the same. The champion gets to pull the lever. Whether she gets coins clattering into the cup below depends a lot on luck. Sophisticated machines allow good progress to be held in one quarter whilst another pull rotates the rest of the fruit.
6. If volume or costs or added value are right, hold that and pull again.

## 4. SHOULD PRIORITIES SET THEMSELVES?

The game can be played with coins and a machine or metaphorically. Childish? Of course. It is a contrivance, as all planning is, to tease out possible actions that would not otherwise come to light. It is no more than an agenda for innovation. It is a simulation of the real world which also encourages managers to associate themselves with those innovations they believe. Everyone plays and no one gets hurt. The objective is to liberate thinking, to make anything seem possible because then perhaps it is.

The meeting, we will suppose, has provided a set of innovations, what is involved, the costs and benefits. Vertical thinking now requires you to set priorities. This may or may not be a good idea. Good, i.e. fired up, champions will ignore them anyway. On the other hand you may need a little more combat to determine true ownership of these ideas. If no one owns them they are unlikely to happen at all. Speed to market has become an imperative as competition hots up. The leisurely days of endless research are gone. Generating enthusiasm and commitment are integral to providing innovation for the ultimate consumer in the shortest possible time.

Setting priorities can provide reasons for delay; it is easier to put things back than forward. Clearly each manager needs to have her own priorities. Only when these compete for resources or depend on others does the need for sequencing arrive.

Back in the office many enthusiasms will wither and die. Some will not. They may need nurture, encouragement, limited funding, testing. That process is not just building individual new ideas into profits but also building the organization's change culture. Innovation is not just allowed but expected as the mainstream of marketing. It is not just for the centre or marketers or R&D or planners but everyone everywhere. In other words, new it all along.

- **MEMO TO FILE**

*Subject:* NEW IT ALL ALONG

- Innovation is the life blood of marketing. Creative ideas are valuable but the greater part is harnessing them to profitable productive change. Brand management needs to ensure that it is organized and rational.

- Wisdom before the event requires participation within a culture of change. Get your team together to review a full agenda for innovation.

- Establish champions or some equivalent 'ownership' of major projects. Major changes need evangelism.

- Do you need priorities? Every individual manager should be pressing forward with innovation, fast. Where priority setting is more likely to delay some than speed others, leave it to reality.

# O

## 17.  Old it right there

**ISSUES:**

1. The importance of heritage for knowing where a brand belongs.
2. Introduce a brand as one would a person: establish shared experience.
3. Then maintain it.

### 1.  BELONGING

Heritage matters to a brand. A traditional category, such as whisky, leads consumers to expect traditional brand values. A modern category, such as electronic audio equipment, may need space age dynamics. The acceptance of the personality of a brand is little different from the acceptance of someone new to a group; the rest of the group will want to know, but may be too polite to ask, about the stranger's position in life, education, current occupation, family and friends.

Before one can come to terms with the individual, we want to know where he or she fits in. We are establishing heritage. For marketers, there is a need to build heritage as well as building the brand itself. This will allow the brand in time to fit comfortably into the consumer's mental portfolio of acceptable brands.

In the world of art, the term for this concept is provenance. Unless we can track the picture from artist, step by step to sale room, authenticity will be in doubt and value reduced.

A new brand in a traditional category is likely to need the same kind of veneer of age as an old master, but the marketer may decide to take the riskier route of obvious contemporaneity. The choice should consciously be between old or bold; which is the better path to consumer acceptance. The brand will need some differentiation, preferably in the product itself; the consumer is being invited to abandon some other tried and trusted brand in favour of the new one, and it may be asking a lot to expect the consumer to accept a novel heritage too. In traditional categories, old is more likely to succeed than bold.

Even in non-traditional categories, a second-hand heritage may still be preferable. The question is still the same. What context can we give the brand personality to help the consumer welcome the new brand into his portfolio? Familiarity can breed consent.

While the introductory phase is crucial, heritage considerations encompass all marketing programmes. The heritage of a brand should never be compromised. A good example is Bombay Gin, the third largest imported gin in the USA and a more vigorous brand than its seniors. It was conceived for the USA market in a Chicago night club at some unmentionable time in the morning. The brand is starting to meet success due to the excellence of the product in other markets too but this is beside the point.

Bombay is packaged to reflect traditional British qualities. There is a picture of Queen Victoria on the label along with a number of symbols of the Raj. No false claims are made; if we the consumers thought about it, the trappings would be clearly trappings. Yet we have no wish to do so for we are participants in the game. In a sense, all the brands we use are our friends. We know some are cheap, some pretentious, some a little out of date, but they are our friends. But as marketers, we have to rationalize that loyalty. In this case the gin is easily distinguishable and has substantive product advantages. The Bombay packaging simply adds value to any display of drinks in the drawing room.

In the USA that packaging is accepted and no longer serves as an introduction. The significance now is that every advertising campaign and every promotion has to fit the personality of the brand and the wider provenance that surrounds it.

Retailers regularly re-create their fascias, logos and other designs to meet the mood of consumer fashion. What is historically accurate blends with what might have been. Chris Macrae (see page 111) recounts that the association of tartans with their clans has little to do with covering the knees of ancient Scots and all to do with a visit of the George IV to Scotland in 1830. The Scots needed instant heritage. Queen Victoria and Walter Scott may have gone on to do more for Scottish history than history ever did.

Marketers tread a careful path in order to maintain both accuracy and shared fantasy without trespassing into deceit. A visitor to London can meet examples all over town; Penhaligons, Richoux, and pubs that were once modern and are now traditional (check if the beams are plastic). If the trend continues, London will become more fictional than Euro-Disney. Crabtree and Evelyn have achieved the same from their USA base. If consumers favour traditional values, marketers simply follow with traditional packaging. If Festival of Britain styling ever comes back into fashion, heaven help us, then expect a rash of businesses proclaiming 'established 1951'.

## 2. INTRODUCING A BRAND

'Old it right there' refers not only to the need for heritage but to the uneasy balance of heritage with innovation. Each marketer has to determine the line between good presentation and manipulation. To select the appropriate clothes for a party is simply good manners. That is presentation. To have people believe one is a bishop when one is not, is manipulative. So can you dress as a bishop at a fancy dress party? Marketing is context specific. It is also subjective. What is manipulation to a consumerist may be presentation to a consumer.

Linking a brand more closely to consumer experience is a valid marketing tool. Every brand introduction should maximize the extent of shared experience. This is why brand extension is so much easier: the heritage and shared experiences are already established. Of course, if the new member of the family turns out to be a black sheep, the rest will suffer.

## 3. MAINTAINING HERITAGE

The consumer is comfortable with the familiar, so why innovate? To meet the consumer's wants, one should continue with whatever now exists. As we saw in the last chapter increasing satiation builds both the demand for innovation and the pace. Yet familiarity has to be maintained.

The brand name, the logo, the use of colours, the style of the advertising supply a large part of that. The trick, perhaps, is to reverse the Salami Principle: instead of taking small slices off quality, add small slices of added values. The added values may be product innovations, heritage, packaging, stories in the press.

Detergents use this technique constantly. When Daz introduced its cheaper refill packs, the benefits were advertised with a hark back to the traditional Daz advertising of yesteryear.

At any point in time the brand should appear to be consistent, familiar and possessed of the same old high standards. Yet at the same time all the while it should be improving its competitive position.

In this marketing paradigm, innovations are focused, one at a time, on where the most improvement can be achieved for the least cost or perceptible change. These elements may not all be reconcilable. If a big fix is needed, then it will have to be provided. The nature of the change will determine whether it should be flagged to the consumer or not. For example, 'New, improved' may be a fine addition to a detergent carton, but not to a bottle of Johnnie Walker Black Label; Johnnie Walker packaging does change, but it does so discreetly.

Whether silent or overt, the change should be narrow, allowing all other components of the brand to retain their familiarity. The marketer may wish to stress either consistency or improvement; yet both are important. In the debates about change, newer managers are classically pitted against those with longer service. To see winners, losers and compromisers as the outcome is wrong. The consumer needs to be resold both what is to be changed and what will stay the same. To do that, stand in the consumer's shoes.

To old it right there is to recognize the importance both of heritage and the strength of the familiar. Introducing the new is also an opportunity to reinforce the old.

● **MEMO TO FILE**

*Subject:* OLD IT RIGHT THERE

● Do not launch a new brand without building the right heritage to make the introduction to the consumer. That is only polite.

● Maintain that heritage consistently through future marketing programmes. From the consumer's view, what feels right?

● Change incrementally in small but frequent steps. Otherwise drastic, and therefore dangerous, measures will become needed. At each step, sell the new within fresh reinforcement of the familiar. Innovation is essential for the future but the old established values pay the bills today.

# Ps and Qs

## 18.  The Ps and Qs of the marketing mix

**ISSUE:**

1.  The basic tools of marketing.

Marketing is the business of innovation. Nowhere does that more apply than the vocabulary. Nothing in hard covers can keep pace with the application of new words to the ancient business of the marketplace. Fundamentalists, meanwhile, plug on with the basic tools of the trade : the Ps and Qs.

Teachers used to follow the 3 Rs immediately with the 4 Ps : product, price, promotion and place. There is still not much wrong with the thought that the right product at the right price with the right place will sell successfully. With time, the number of Ps has expanded. The correct sequence is debatable but the chapters used here are:

- Positioning
- Product and packaging
- Pricing
- Promotion and advertising
- Public relations
- Personal selling
- Place – here replaced by 'Distribution channels'

Together these ingredients, 'the marketing mix', make up the market plan, which has a chapter to itself.

The Qs of marketing fundamentalism are quantity and quality. Britain traditionally viewed those as trade offs. Consumers could choose one or the other. One can attribute British twentieth century commercial failure to many roots but the inability to recognize, as the Japanese did, that quality and quantity can reinforce one another is certainly one.

Positioning is a concept which has been reinvented several times. It refers to the way consumers see the bundle of images and product values that make up a brand in relation to its competitors. What is the central Proposition of a brand? What is its Personality? How will it differentiate itself from competition? And how will it gain advantage? How Premium or Prestigious is it? Sun Tzu used the concept over 2,000 years ago. Ries and Trout redefined it in 1980s. You may as well Position your own.

Products and their packaging are not identical to brands. One brand may have many products. The same product may appear as different brands. A brand will have intangible personality attributes over and above the physical goods or services that make up the product.

Pricing is a subject that has whole books and term long courses to itself. The premium a brand secures over the equivalent product may indicate the strength of the brand provided sales or share are also strong. Price drives profit and brand equity more directly than any other component of the marketing mix. Pricing thus serves both as a measure of quality to the consumer and, given robust sales, of marketing success.

Promotion is a word of ambiguity. Too often it means discounting. Non-price promotions now have to be separated out. A product manager knows promotion means more power, authority and premium when it applies to his job. It is a pity the same thinking does not apply to the brands to which it is applied. Advertising, also known as 'above the line', has its own chapter.

Public relations to some is the poor relation of the marketing but others treat it as the linchpin for building consumer word of mouth and respect.

Personal selling is the infantry work of marketing. Sometimes undervalued, Passion for the brand delivers results one step at a time. Particularly critical in the early stages of a brand's existence, it supplies the feedback from the marketplace enabling the necessary changes to be made. Some companies now see selling as the setting up of Partner relationships with customers, distributors and also inside the company itself.

Place (also know as Point of Sale or more commonly now, Point of Purchase, POS or POP) has been included as distribution channels because one needs to review the whole sequence from producer to consumer, not just the final retail shelf.

With these tools, roughly in the order they are used, in the bag, you will be ready to go back to work. Putting them together, or synthesis, is Planning, itself a framework for innovation. A plan only needs to be formalized as a document when a team is involved and agreement needs to be reached in such a way that it can be reviewed in the future. Planning is simply part of the corporate learning process which cycles round, usually annually, through implementation, measurement of results and then their analysis.

Knowing the Ps and Qs, in whatever modern terminology, is only a few steps away from the souk trader who says 'Please' with such conviction that your wallet opens itself. Or is that one P word too many ?

# 19.  Positioning – The martial art of marketing

**ISSUES:**

1. Differentiating the brand and establishing preference.
2. Defining the target consumer.
3. Perceptual maps and other mind pictures.
4. Using oriental lessons in strategy.

## 1.  BRAND DIFFERENTIATION AND PREFERENCE

The value of a brand is created by consumers in their own minds. Constant rediscovery of this old idea is witness to its vitality. Positioning is the art of putting it there. Repositioning is locating where that brand's persona fits relative to competitors and moving it towards the ideal. Fanciful? Difficult certainly. A consumer's mindset, even if it could be so accurately determined, changes with mood, experience and competing needs. Consumers differ (yes, really!). Yet asking a marketing manager about the current positioning of the brand and how it should be changed, should be like turning on a tap. Try it.

Some marketers believe that positioning is not a matter of imagery but substantive product characteristics. Cars with larger engines are positioned apart from those with lower horse power.

Real product advantages are always preferable to pure images. In practice marketers need all the help they can get, i.e. both.

A brand is a brand because it is different to other brands. The positioning statement differentiates the brand and shows how it is, or will be, preferred.

Positioning is one of those occasional exercises, once every five years, say, that must be right because all marketing activities should flow from it, consistently.

## 2. THE TARGET CONSUMER

It begins with the target consumer. Whose preference is being sought? To see the product through consumer eyes, one has to know whose eyes they are supposed to be. Well established brands may be targeted at the whole population. More often a particular segment is selected and then enlarged once success is achieved. Segmentation allows marketing to be more accurately directed and resources better focused.

A mature brand may have its strength with an aging consumer group. Should one reposition the brand to appeal to younger and more affluent consumers? If so, how can one avoid alienating those now providing the cash flow? The traditional consumer description was in demographic terms: age, sex, family size and socio-economic class. The UK tended to simplify 'class' to occupation or spending power: A and B for higher and middle, C1 for white collar office workers, C2 for blue collar, D for minimum waged and E for the rest. With A only representing 2 per cent of the population it was lumped with B. As blue collar working is progressively taken over by mechanization, the coarse grain of this analysis is of diminishing value: it really was there just to make the media buyers' lot easier. As the media categorized their readers or viewers in that way, the media buyer knew what to look for. In terms of significant disposable income, there are mostly only two groups now, AB and C, too coarse an analysis for sensitive segmentation.

The USA uses rather more specific breaks of earning levels, education, ethnic and occupation groups. Such groups are easy to identify with and to research but the format says little about the behaviour characteristics of the target.

In the 1970s attempts were made to supplement these demographic classifications with psychographics, i.e. personality and behaviour characteristics. The marketer was glad to deal with portraits of real, or more real, people. Measurement became more expensive and less reliable. Does measurement matter? It is true that empathy is the most beneficial result from a clearer picture of the consumer and that this does not need quantification. On the other hand, the size of the segment, how much they spend on the category and competitor shares all feed into the planning process.

Early psychographic measurement suffered from subjectivity and variation. Each researcher created different segment definitions. When we describe our own personalities and ways of life on questionnaires, how accurate and truthful are we? Over the next ten years, researchers codified their practices and tested them from country to country. What they did was to compute huge volumes of psychographic data to produce clusters of consumer groups that would behave consistently, from time to time, country to country, product group to product group.

These methodologies are branded in different ways. Sometimes the same product is used with different names by different advertising agencies. Branding again. A classic 'VALS' (Value And Life Styles) was invented by SRI International to distinguish nine psychographic clusters of consumers. It was used by one of the leading worldwide advertising agencies, Young & Rubicam, at the time of the 1987 UK general election. Politicians are chary of admitting to their increasing use of marketing techniques because few of us like being marketed at. Y&R did not allow its subsidiaries around the world to take part in political activities but had no objection to its executives doing so, using agency data but on their own account. Y&R had been tracking the ratings of the political parties in the run up to the election. The full story has yet to be told but it has been alleged that the election outcome depended on a late shift in strategy brought about by a different view of consumer preferences. Y&R executives were providing a VALS based analysis directly to 10 Downing Street whilst Conservative Central Office were using different, more traditional sources. The greater sensitivity of the VALS psychographic information reinforced the Prime Minister's concerns with the direction of the campaign and enabled her to make the necessary changes to win.

Positioning needs a clear stereotype of the target consumer. Some brand managers find likenesses in magazines and pin them on their walls. At least that was who they said they were. A single picture can tell your copywriter more than a page of analysis even if the market researcher does want it in VALS.

## 3. PERCEPTUAL MAPS

Better to be fixated by the consumer's relationship with your brand than with competition. That intensity of focus allows one to see what others miss. Why else are garrets so productive for artists? Excessive concern with competition is distracting and enfeebling. If the consumer-brand relationship is strong enough, there is nothing to worry about. If it is weak then it is that relationship that has to be strengthened. The consumer and the brand are two people that the marketer, as matchmaker, is trying to get to love one another. Presenting the best features of one to the other tends to work better than trying to alienate the consumer from other suitors. For positioning we need to know who and where the competitors are, mostly to stay out of their way. Before we do anything we need a map.

Mapping the consumers' minds may sound millenial, the maths a bit advanced, but the process is simple enough. What do consumers want and how well does each brand deliver each attribute?

In 1970 the UK target vodka consumer wanted first purity or cleanliness of spirit, then potency and then a whole list of attributes with diminishing enthusiasm. 'Smoothness' is one of the most demanded characteristics of spirit drinks. Vodka was able to go further and offer alcohol with almost no impurities. On the face of it, purity and smoothness were the strongest potential claims. Potency was interesting because vodka was perceived to be stronger than other spirits such as whisky, gin or rum whereas, in reality, it was 6.5 per cent weaker.

Having established what the attributes are, the consumer can tell you how each brand rates on that scale. This is where the mathematics come in. There can be a lot of attributes. The most important to the consumer may not be actionable to the marketer because all brands rate the same. One can either consider the most actionable and forget the rest or one can apply factor or cluster analysis to reduce the number of attributes to understandable size. Better still, draw the positions on maps. Using purity and potency as two dimensions for example, the 1970 vodka market could have been mapped like this:

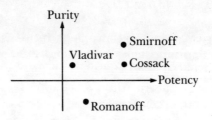

*Figure 11   The Vodka market, 1970*

We now have a map of where the brands lie. We also know where the ideal position is though there may be conflicts, e.g. wanting the most expensive brand at the cheapest price. In addition to marking the positions the map can indicate the strength of each brand. The perfect positioning is the point on the map representing the ideal from the target consumer's point of view which is also furthest away from the competition, especially the strong competition.

Even if you like this technique, and quite a few marketers do not, perfect positioning rarely exists. The usual choice is between over-competitive positions and those empty spaces that are empty for good reason – the consumer does not like it. Neither will really do but by reviewing the maps, consumer segment by segment, a least bad position can be identified where there is a chance of brand differentiation in ways attractive to the consumer.

An alternative is to use associations by 'projecting' brands onto some totally different species, animals for example, or even different religions. Whatever methodology is used, the outcome needs to be a clear picture of how the brand and its competitors relate to consumers' wishes, how they are apart from one another and where the preferences lie. We have now arrived at the fun, the point at which positioning becomes a martial art. You know where the players are. How are you going to move?

## 4.   USING ORIENTAL LESSONS IN STRATEGY

The players in this game are the consumer, the competitors and you. You want to win. You have less resources than you think you need. Your budget has been cut. Life was ever thus. There are many books on strategy from Sun Tzu's *Art of War/Strategy* through Clausewitz to whichever General has most recently written his memoirs.

Perhaps the greatest of these in modern times is Mao Tse Tung. His chronicles of the long marches are not just one of the definitive works of guerilla warfare but also a marketing manual. Communism as a brand was not particularly attractive to the Chinese. Sun Yat Sen had been using apparently similar ideologies to undermine the Imperial order for the previous 50 years. In reality he had just been the front for gangster elements. The corruption of the old order was replaced by the corruption of the, supposedly socialist, new. In any case the Utopian ideals of communism fitted the agrarian, individual and commercial characteristics of the Chinese rather poorly.

There are no rules in marketing because established rules would become boring for the consumer, especially after they were imitated by competitors. It is absurd to paraphrase major works into a few sentences and expect to retain meaning. Disregarding such *caveats*, here are a few of the lessons arising:

1. Only go where the competitor is if you will crush him. If he is bigger than you are, go some place else.
2. Gain strength by cooperating with competitors in the short term. Helping them at their own expense reduces the apparent threat and builds your resources for the day you can strike decisively. Joint ventures are a valuable source of learning.

3. If he is big and trampling out new territory, he is probably making nice places for you. It may be worth following at a discreet distance.

4. If competitors are fighting each other, leave them to it.

5. Find out which way the wind is blowing, i.e. trends. Lighting a small fire upwind of consumers enables you to wait for smoke to give cover for your moves and your words to drift down to them. Downwind you will always be too visible and too late. (Unfortunately, downwind movements look trendy to management and are easier to get accepted.)

6. Do not do for consumers what they can do for themselves. For example if your product is pale in colour, do not waste money telling them what they can see.

7. Be as visible to the consumer as you are opaque to the competition.

8. Do not make your plan obvious. If you do not know what you are doing either, it may even help.

9. When the fantasizing is all done, positioning must be realistic. A brand can only be, and should only try to be, what it is. A façade cannot be defended for long. Positioning is making the best of what a brand is, not trying to be something else.

How did the positioning exercise work for Smirnoff in 1970? Purity was the key attribute but it was decided not to go for it. Other vodkas, mostly Cossack at that time, did the same research and tended to major on purity. Consumers knew vodka was relatively pure anyway. They also knew that Smirnoff was more expensive and therefore, by inference, better. The perception that vodka was stronger than it really was, was the key fact. So was Russian-ness. There were associations with large, husky men in furs and spurs downing glasses in one and throwing them into fireplaces whilst blondes fainted. The label showed clearly that Smirnoff was made in England. Many knew that it came from Harlow, Essex. They preferred to enjoy the myth. Potency was where Smirnoff positioned itself. Over the decade sales grew from about 300,000 cases a year to over two million.

- **MEMO TO FILE**

*Subject:* POSITIONING

- Positioning is the art of establishing the brand in the minds of the target consumers most advantageously relative to competition. Positioning uses both real and image attributes.

- That requires total understanding of the stereotypical target consumer, your own brand and the relationship between them. Do not try to be what your brand is not nor what the consumer finds incredible. A durable relationship requires realism.

- It also requires understanding of competitor positionings but do not be mesmerized by them.

- Let your brand's weakness take advantage of competitive strengths. Use the oriental strategic arts as a guide. Only compete on winning terms. The rest of the time, cooperate or stay clear.

# 20.  Products and Packaging

**ISSUES:**

1.  Need for verifiable product advantage – the USP or product differentiation.
2.  Need for consistency.
3.  The use of packaging to invigorate branding.
4.  Product or Brand Life Cycles.
5.  Durables.

## 1.  DIFFERENTIATION

There is much confusion between the terms *brand* and *product*. Which is the hero and which the afterthought? Is a product different from a service? They *are* different, and have existences semi-independent of one another. A product may be either a solid object or a service, something sold to a consumer or to another business. The distinction between services and physical goods is not as great as is generally supposed. Services have some tangible form; a bank provides statements and a consultant a report. The supplier of goods usually offers services. In marketing terms, they can both be treated as products.

The product consists of all those utilitarian attributes the rational consumer gets for his or her money. They include technical and economic benefits: with a car, for example, benefits include fuel economy and space for passengers and freight. 'Product' here excludes those more ephemeral qualities of brand personality, consumer perceptions and psycho-social benefits which add value to the product from the consumer's point of view. Packaging is simply the external skin of the product that the buyer sees; in the case of a service, packaging refers to the appearance of sales staff, paper, shop fascias or whatever the user encounters. Thus:

$$\text{Product} + \text{Packaging} + \text{Added Value} = \text{Brand}$$

Vodka, the product, is pure ethyl alcohol ($C_2O_5OH$) mixed with water. It is, in the purest practical sense, useful for removing stains from ties but not much else. Virtually all of those lovely qualities that create demand and satisfaction are in the mind; to proclaim the chemical formulae to be reality and dismiss the intangible attributes as irrelevant fantasy would be throwing a diamond ring out with the potato peelings.

Nevertheless, product and packaging differences do matter. It may seem eccentric to have to mention that, but previous generations of marketers became so absorbed with images that reality was left behind. Their successors believe that the product itself now matters more than ever. Any substantive advantage a physical product or a service can gain over the competition will help sales now and long after competition has caught up in real terms. Product advantage lingers in the sub-memory. Of all the promises the consumers receives, this one is the most concrete and tangible.

Procter & Gamble has traditionally insisted on verifiable product advantage before any new product is launched. That is an admirable spur to R&D and marketers alike. Large or small, these advantages give the salesman a difference worth talking about and reassurance to the rational part of the customer's intellect. Whatever our true reason for buying, we like to be able to justify our choice.

In the case of vodka, Smirnoff is filtered through nine

columns of activated charcoal and emerges cleaner and purer. No other vodka follows that process. The difference is subtle and immensely uninteresting. To the modern consumer when Smirnoff was first introduced, the difference mattered. An acceptance that product quality has been demonstrated still supports the brand today.

Rosser Reeves coined the expression Unique Selling Proposition (USP) in the 1930s. One of the founders of the Ted Bates advertising agency, Reeves was dedicated to the idea that the product must have a difference, preferably a verifiable advantage, and it should be used consistently in all advertising. For him, the medium was not the message. Marketing trends took that idea in and out of fashion but Reeves was fundamentally right. Sales forces the world over have reason to be grateful for his championing such a primitive thought: give us something we can tell our customers. (Now that 'USP' is passé, 'Product Differentiation' is used to mean the same thing).

Maintaining commitment to discernible product advantage is tough, especially when everyone knows that the principal action will lie in the intangibles. It is doubly difficult to provide product advantage in services where the key factor is inter-personal contact; it is hard to brand people. One can provide uniforms, or send the entire workforce to a standardized charm school as British Airways did in 1989. Total Quality Management is a vital part of industrial and services marketing. Some cultures adapt to it more readily than others; it will be interesting to see if Euro-Disney can hold to the same standardized product as in Florida and California. Marks & Spencer recruit to tight guidelines so that their culture can be perpetuated and reproduced in all stores. The more characteristics are shared by all staff, the easier it is to present a consistent service product.

Consistency is fundamental to branding and therefore to products. The simpler a service product can be made, the easier it is to achieve consistency. This was once true for physical goods too; only relatively simple objects, soap for example, could be branded. As technology advanced so did consistency and the opportunity for branding. The development of technology in the service arena is following, with similar branding opportunities. Some institutions have managed over the years to brand themselves; Oxford and Cambridge have for years been leading brands in higher education.

So far we have considered a product and a brand having a one-on-one relationship. In practice a single brand can cover many products, each of which may appear in different sizes, shapes and forms. Conversely a single product may appear as different brands. This is a device for segmenting customers and/or consumers. The extension of contraction of brands with more or less products is discussed in the chapter on 'Brand Equity'.

Now, after the flirtation with fantasy in the 1970s and 80s, recession has refocused on the products themselves. There has been a revival of interest in quality both of goods and services. This too has its own chapter. The topics we should review now are:

- Better quality is important but so is consistency.
- Is packaging just a way to stop the product falling off the shelf?
- Brand and Product Life Cycles : Facts or Fantasies ?

## 2.  IMPORTANCE OF BEING CONSISTENT

The story is told of the newly appointed managing director of a famous Scotch whisky company crossing the Atlantic by sea in the early 60s. He was delighted to hear a wealthy American call loudly for his brand in the bar each evening. By day four, he felt he had to introduce himself to his enthusiastic consumer. 'Why is this your favourite whisky?' 'It isn't', came the reply, 'I'm just fascinated by the way every bottle is different.'

Customers like that are even fewer than variable whiskies. A brand name is a mnemonic for a bundle of expected attributes. In this rushed age, the consumer does not have time to stop and think. The name bubbles up to consciousness, and it is assumed the product will be the same as last time. And it had better be.

For the world-wide marketer this can be a problem. Over the years products and packaging may have been adapted to local market preferences. Now, global marketing has arrived.

Whether consumers really worry about their favourite brand tasting different in one market to another is unclear; management does. The drive is on to standardize and upgrade packaging, to improve consistency.

## 3. PACKAGING

In this self-service age, packaging is too important to be considered an afterthought: for first purchases, the packaging is the most immediate feature of the brand. Some go so far as to propose that the package be designed before the product; if the package must communicate to the buyer what lies inside, then why not to the producers also? Whilst that may be extreme, there are cases where the package made the brand. Long Life, for example, was the first UK canned beer. The package dictated both the necessary qualities of the product and the way it was marketed. Deodorants likewise developed from the spray can. However, technical packaging advantage evaporates even more quickly than product advantage because packaging suppliers immediately widen their market to their other customers.

The trend to added value, better quality without necessarily more volume, applies both to both product and packaging. Packaging has to carry the product in every sense. The paper label of yesterday will not do for the consumer of tomorrow. With fragmented media, there is no certainty the consumer will have seen whatever advertising is current; with a major fmcg launch, usually only about 20 per cent of first-time purchasers have any awareness of advertising. One must work on the basis that the package is the only communication about the brand and the product the consumer will receive.

The designer has an unenviable role. The package must keep the product in shape and in good condition. It must withstand transportation and handling. Legal and technical words and numbers must be easy to read. The branding must be overt, and yet sometimes discreet as well. Colours must reflect the brand as it has always been, and yet be modern and fashionable. The package must communicate prestige and value for money. It has to shout 'buy me' from the shelf but then merge gently into the decor when you get it home. And do not forget the bar and universal product codes. It is little wonder that a package designer needs a clear idea of what the brand is trying to achieve. Must the pack be a can? Must it be cylindrical? When the background is in place, the limits to creativity need to be probed. Good designers shock complaisant clients. The colour of the client's neck is an index of creativity. However, this should be the most enjoyable part of the process for the marketer. If the technical experts are not showing signs of alarm, maybe you have the wrong designer.

When the feathers have unruffled, the designer should leave with a written brief, signed by all. The objectives should leave no room for doubt. Less popular with designers, and often counter-productive, is advice from the client on how the problem can be solved.

## Repackaging

Repackaging can invigorate tired products. It can motivate sales forces and customers. It can upstage the competition. All it takes is imagination, vision and enough of a budget to hire top talent and execute a solution without scrimping. That looks wonderful on paper, but top talent and no scrimping is a formula for spending more money than is available. But vision and imagination, at least, are free. A clear direction helps, even if the money is not there. The conventional wisdom is that packaging changes should be small and frequent rather than large and occasional. There are always exceptions. If your brand has a severe image problem, a more drastic solution is required. In this case it might be best to issue shock-proof clothing to all senior members of the team, particularly those with responsibility for budgets.

Maintenance is not expensive if it is regular and well done. Otherwise it simply becomes essential. A rare outburst of tact withholds the name of the brand to which this conversation refers:

'Brand X is in severe need of repackaging.'

*'I agree.'*

'When will it be done?'

*'When we can afford it.'*
'When will that be?'
*'When sales pick up.'*

The budgetary issue should be an irrelevance: repackaging must earn its keep.

The role of packaging in revitalizing products is more likely to grow than lessen, especially as the other 'Ps' of the marketing mix achieve diminishing returns. There are limits to how much better some products can get, and to how much more they can charge. Promotions beyond a point become counter-productive. Advertising has so many media, so many impressions, so much regulation, so much inflation that its value has been eroded. Packaging has one supreme advantage as a communicator: if the consumer is near enough to read it, she is near enough to buy it. A pack in the hand is worth two on the shelf.

## 4.   LIFE CYCLES: FACTS OR FANTASIES?

Re-invigorating products challenges one of the great marketing phantoms: the Life Cycle. The very name conjures up eternal verities, or maybe technology in a health spa. Either way, one is expected to believe in the Brand or Product Life Cycle, one of those marketing myths that seem to prove themselves. The theory goes like this: where there is life, there is death. It is the natural order. Since brands and products are created, so must they die. Marketers should maximize their profits by following the natural cycle. (See Figure 12)

Such strategies are likely to be self-fulfilling. As soon as a downturn is interpreted as a Life Cycle decline, the brand or product is prepared for the mortuary. The theory is compounded by the analysis of consumers into separate segments of innovators, early adopters, early majority, late majority and laggards. Originally just statistics, such concepts have been refined with rigor mortis. As brands or products move from niche to mass markets, the theory goes, the innovators become bored and switch. By the time the laggards are catching on, the early adopters have left too. The Life Cycle, a form of fashion, inevitably follows its natural course.

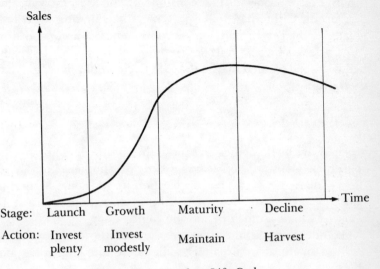

Figure 12   Product Life Cycle

As a general theorem this is piffle. Brands can survive for ever by changing the products under their umbrellas. Brands of soap have become detergents and then biological detergents leading to concentrates. Perhaps Life Cycles apply to products not brands? What about salt? Brands and products survive until something better takes their place. Life Cycles do indeed appear to apply to durables or other products which are not consumed. (See below). Innovators may move to more fashionable products but they, or their children, can also return. Brands and products do not necessarily die. They do so when mismanaged, or when supplanted by a better solution to consumer needs.

To believe in the Life Cycle is to cause it to happen. It is not unusual for brands to reach a plateau before rising again, but the Life Cycle chartist will see a plateau as prelude to decline. Baileys Irish Cream had a dramatically fast climb in most countries where it was launched between 1974 and 1980. Cynics forecast, using the same natural metaphors, that mushroom growth would lead to equally fast decline. When sales levelled off, the tea trolleys were taking round tranquillizers. With hindsight it was obvious that consumers were indeed trying the new products that had followed Baileys but, finding them less palatable, had returned. Sales continued upwards and the Life Cycle was forgotten. If any of those follower products really had been better, then maybe the Life Cycle would have 'proved' itself again.

## 5. DURABLES

Much of this book focuses on brands the consumer continuously consumes. Consumption leaves space for another. Life Cycle theory does have greater application to durables. Once a houseperson has an oven it will be a long time before it is replaced unless a much better one comes along.

The diffusion of innovation, i.e. the spread of new products, follows, for durables, a pattern akin to the Life Cycle diagram above.

*Figure 13    Diffusion of Innovation – Durables*

Whatever the point at which the new product plateaus out, the plateau will bring a decline in sales until a substantial technological breakthrough appears: colour TV to follow black and white, digital text, high definition and so on. Marketers of durables and other products which are not consumed need to know where they are on the cycle and adapt their policies accordingly.

Inertia brings equal dangers, yet surely products and packaging cannot be constantly changed. There are other things to do, and consistency matters too. Always improving, always standardizing and attending to the rest of the marketing mix at the same time is a formula riddled with contradictions. Nevertheless, Japanese high tech companies manage to do it. Can you?

- **MEMO TO FILE**

*Subject:* PRODUCTS AND PACKAGING

- Differentiate or die. Secure verifiable product advantage where you can. Even when competition catches up, the perception should linger.

- Quality matters and that includes consistency. Variations from market to market need a strong rationale. Continuous small improvement should converge market-to-market differences toward common excellence.

- Forget Life Cycles except for durables. Products die when they are mismanaged or the market-place gets a better offer. Products that deliver what the brand promises will live as long as they are delivering the best.

- Marketers of durables and other non-consumable products do need to understand the diffusion of innovation and adapt policies to where their products stand. To perpetuate brands, new products need to fit the cycles.

- Re-packaging invigorates and revitalizes. Packaging can add value, and it may be the primary vehicle for consumer communication. Packaging may also supply the verifiable advantage you are seeking. Is your packaging working hard enough?

# 21. Pricing in grandmother's footsteps

**ISSUES:**

1. Price is the litmus test of marketing. Not just the key link to profit but premium is a key indicator of brand strength.
2. Before deciding strategy assert basic controls to see the whole picture.
3. Classic pricing trouble spots.
4. Invisible pricing strategies.

## 1. THE LITMUS TEST

Pricing can be simple or incomprehensible or both. Many professionals just follow the brand leader or, as brand leader, move prices up whenever the competition is likely to follow. Too superficial to win Oscars from economists, this policy still makes money. At the other extreme lie sophisticated computer simulations of industry-customer relationships. In between lie the serpentine contortions businesses bring to pricing and discounting. Houdini was an apprentice pricing manager before he decided to go straight.

Without special offers, price wars, coupons and the myriad devices for giving the consumer her money back, bargains would not seem like bargains nor shopping so complex. Many famous grocery brands in the USA today never sell except on offer. Consumers can live by deals alone. Even if the consumer inadvertently buys at full price, the retailer will still claim the discount from the brand owner if he can get away with it.

Any marketer who initiates money-off schemes, without thinking through the consequences, is crazy. Many of the schemes are crazy, period. There are signs that marketers, customers and consumers are tiring of them. Tactical discounting and promotions will retain their roles in the marketer's toolkit because craziness in moderation is good. But such methods should be secondary to the main business of building brands.

Pricing is central to marketing in many ways. It communicates positioning to consumer and customer alike and therefore must reinforce the competitive stance the marketer wishes to adopt. A premium price signifies quality – providing quality has been achieved. A premium also signifies brand strength, differentiation and consumer preference.

Price is conventionally seen as a trade with volume: the higher the price, the lower the volume. This is not always the case. The method, frequency and timing of price changes can produce different volume results for any given ultimate price change. Some dispute this and believe that price elasticity is constant, the same price change will have the same volume result however you get there. In particular circumstances, a price increase will stimulate **more** volume if it signals higher quality.

What are we trying to achieve with pricing? The consumer should be able to buy at a price which maximizes the brand owner's profit over time and is consistent with the positioning of the brand. Consistency is a principle reason for brand loyalty. Rapid changes of pricing unsettle the consumer. When the current spate of 'deals' recedes, loyalty will be rocked for the opposite reason: the consumer has come to expect regular price dips and surges on certain brands and will be unsettled when they cease.

Nothing, not even volume, translates to the bottom line as quickly as price. The chart above shows a classic price volume

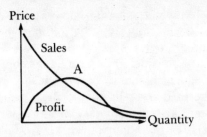

*Figure 14  Prices and volumes*

relationship and the consequential profits and losses. To choose price point A appears to maximize profit: something like this appears in every text book, but beware. Such analysis is simplistic.

For a start, it ignores the downstream effects as the brand moves through the distribution channel: how will each customer choose to pass prices on to the next until the eventual consumer price is reached? It ignores discounting and tactical offers which shift sales from period to period. How will that affect the calculation? How will competitors react? If different competitors have different price structures in different markets, how can one match them all and yet prevent products leaching from the intended market to others? How will consumer repeat purchases be affected? How will prices affect long term brand image? How will short term pricing affect the ability to price up in the future?

Such analysis also ignores the impact of inflation which, to some extent, carries pricing along in its own stream. Pricing strategies for no, low, medium and hyper-inflation environments will be totally different. In some ways medium inflation provides the easiest cover for marketers: over-pricing can be corrected by pausing a while.

The analysis also omits price segmentation, perhaps the biggest area for profits growth in the next decade. The ability to price differentially to each cluster of consumers allows the profit to be maximized separately for each segment which, mathematically, automatically maximizes total profit. In global terms, countries can be seen as segments. Brand prices have varied from market to market. With international arbitrage (or the 'grey' or 'parallel') markets freely available, differential pricing by country is diminishing but more sophisticated means of segmentation are being developed.

Price cannot be considered as a single number but as a chain of links each of which can stretch. Each link is the price for which one intermediary sells to the next on the way to the consumer. When each segment has a different set of prices, each brand has as many price chains. Every chain is intertwined with those of competing brands. All are floating along in multi-currency estuaries moving with the tides of inflation. If that is clear, you will not have any more trouble with pricing. Forget simplistic price volume charts, mug up on the microbiology of DNA and go for the Nobel prize on the meaning of price.

Pricing in the real world has more variables than the mind can consider at once. We are rightly suspicious of computer systems that claim to do so. As a result, very few sophisticated models are in use. Most people keep as many variables constant as they can (i.e. match competition) in order to control those few that do move. Even so, the effects are not always those which were intended. In a large company different managers may be changing different variables without full understanding of what others are doing.

Price is the litmus test of successful marketing because it is directly linked to the short- and long-term profitability of the brand. It shows strength or weakness, confidence or timidity, control or confusion. Price is the biggest component of brand equity. It reflects added value and brand differentiation.

## 2.  BASIC CONTROLS: WHO IS REALLY SETTING PRICES?

In the cool carpeted offices of Megabrand Global, all these pricing variables are modelled electronically. Sensors in the marketplace instantly pick up changes in competitor, customer and consumer pricing and behaviour. Price elasticity is the measure developed by economists to relate incremental changes in price with their effects on volume. Megabrand's computer calculates elasticities and cross elasticities (one brand's movement affects another's) and indicates sales responses to forecasts, marginal costs in response to different volumes. Market shares gains are being balanced against profits for the short and long term. All the myriad complexities of pricing can be reconciled by information technology. Paperless presentations flash directly to screens, committees decide and the sales force have something exciting to tell their customers.

All that is possible, but it is largely fantasy. Megabrand is back to the basics of management and responsibilities. With the focus on profit accountability, pricing responsibility has had to be delegated. Can sales be responsible for deals failing if they cannot deal? The growing power of retailers shifted control of marketing budgets to sales management. The extent can be greater than top management realize. One of the major drinks multinationals found that their managers had nearly a hundred different ways of giving money to customers in the EC alone. The study took a year to complete because so many words for 'discount' do not translate; or so the local managers claimed.

In the US foods business, price discounting typically required 15 – 40 per cent of the brand budget in the early 70s. Today it may run as high as 80 per cent. Retailers terrorize suppliers with delisting, 'slotting fees' (to buy spaces on the shelves) and de-slotting fees (to pay the cost of taking your brand off the shelves/retailer's computer). A constant stream of promotions (i.e. tactical discounts) is necessary to maintain visibility, velocity (rate of sale) and competitive edge. With profit margins as low as 1 or 2 per cent, retailers insist that such tactics are necessary for survival. They may weaken the brands on which retailers ultimately survive but they need blood money now.

Loss of control of pricing is not only due to the growing strength of retailers but the complexity of multinational business structures. Accounting systems, in large organizations, may not always be capturing the full picture. The marketing budgets are clear enough but how many companies net discounts off from sales before recording turnover in value terms? In an age where price lists are entered for fiction prizes, what really is the price? There are volume discounts, drop size allowances, dealer loaders, bonuses, inventory equalization offsets, merchandising support, annual rebates, loyalty bonuses, prompt payment or cash with order allowances. In a large organization, each department wants to influence customer behaviour to make that department's operation more efficient. Over time one arrangement piles on another until few (in some companies, no one) can understand what is happening in total, still less the effect on profit.

The sophistication of computer models is less relevant when the emphasis is on acquiring management control. The aim today is to recover control over pricing without losing the flexibility of local dealing. Nowhere is this truer than in the Europe of 1992. Retailers can buy in the EC country of their choice. They can join together to exchange buying information or buy jointly. Brussels, in trying to maximize prices for the farmer whilst minimizing consumer prices, has to squeeze everything in between. A blind eye will therefore be turned to the growing strength of retailers. Who cares about retail competition if the consumer is getting a better deal?

German supermarkets are an education in retailer power. As 1992 approached, it dawned on marketers that their whole European profitability was being dictated by a handful of supermarket groups. Unless firm action was taken, every retailer in Europe would be buying on German terms. In different ways successful marketers are regaining control.

Strategically, pricing should interpret the positioning of the brand on the customers' shelves and in the minds of consumers.

The issue facing brand marketers today is recovering the initiative from retailers and, sometimes, from other parts of their own organizations. This is not an issue for small companies with little competitive freedom nor many managers in the loop. But any multinational should realize that it has problems reconciling local and global/regional pricing and profit responsibilities, problems with sharing information and competitive intelligence.

If it does not, sell your shares. The cliff lies just ahead.

## 3. CLASSIC TROUBLE SPOTS

Computers have not solved any problems. They have just

quickened the pace. Competition sees tactical pricing as a game of poker and raises the ante that much faster. Reaction times are so quick that they can hit the street almost when you do. The coupon craze in the US alcoholic drinks business was an example. Product managers discovered that you could give $1 off the next purchase and economically drive up today's sales. Most coupons were not cashed. Those that were built brand loyalty, or at least the next sale. Furthermore you could give lower prices to those concerned with price and not waste money on the price insensitive consumers. Salesmen liked them because they built a relationship with the retailers.

Competitors joined in. Most brands began to have coupons, the stakes in alcoholic drinks rose from $1 to $2 to $5 or more a bottle. At one point, coupon value equalled the price of the bottle; wine was being given away free. Off licence stores looked like Fifth Avenue after a ticker tape parade. As fast as salesmen put their coupons on top of their competitors', consumers threw them on the ground. Worse still, they began to cash them. Almost as quickly as they appeared, coupons in the US alcoholic drinks business began to disappear.

Giving money away is crazy because the competition need little encouragement to do it too. Everyone loses money and it cheapens the brand in the eyes of the consumer. Marketing should be the business of adding value, not subtracting it. Some idiots still believe one can lose money on every case but make it up on volume. For the sane, tactical dealing and discounting is an important but dangerous tool to be used with discretion.

The risks are clear. So is the strategic requirement that pricing reinforces the positioning of the brand. Supposing all those have been straightened out, and perhaps even if they have not, what then? Faced by the complexities there is always a temptation to do nothing. Why change prices if that will simply provoke competition? This may indeed be the best short term tactic, but not for ever. Procrastination leads eventually to a need to hike prices substantially.

The premium that genuinely better quality deserves should be flagged. A major new competitor or new technology offering much lower prices needs prompt response. Failure to keep up with inflation can be lethal. Pricing on the basis of costs rather than the marketplace reflects lack of customer understanding. To mark up rather than to market is craven.

Although small steps and following competitors may generally be wise, the marketer also needs to know when to be bold.

## 4. INVISIBLE PRICING STRATEGIES

As a general rule (and there are no general rules) pricing strategy should be confident, strong and invisible. Complete invisibility is impossible. The word is used to stress the virtues of consistency, moving with inflation, avoiding the attention of competitors and discretion. This section will review four such pricing strategies:

1. Skimming. Used for new brands with a view to establishing a premium image and then broadening the market and production progressively as the price is brought down.
2. Penetration. Roughly the opposite: a low price is used for rapid expansion to minimize competitor entry or reaction.
3. Retaliating first. When there is strong reason to expect strong, lower priced competition, such as when a patent expires, the evidence is that pre-emptive action is more effective than too little too late.
4. The first three are all special cases dealing with market entries or strategic shifts. 'Paradigm shifts' if you prefer. 'Grandmother's footsteps' is proposed as the most useful day to day model.

### Skimming

The idea that consumers prefer price decreases to increases leads to a strategy of feeling one's way down to the correct price from above. In times of inflation this can be achieved more subtly by allowing the market to catch up. In the same way it may be better to increase the scale of production as manufacturing skills improve. Establishing as much premium as the brand will bear is helpful to brand equity. Competitors are less likely to react to the higher prices and lower volumes. Investment may be less and profits more immediate. Indeed everything is rosy save two snags. Depending on the product category, immediate volume may be critical. So may competitor reaction.

High fashion products such as the hula hoop will sell all they will ever sell within the first year. The production process may have high economies of scale; the marginal costs of production may be low but the fixed costs high. Going for large early volumes in this event is less risky. Retailers may simply block entry to anything that does not offer a fast enough rate of sale (velocity).

The British have a history of producing fine inventions, jet planes for example, in a niche way only to have foreign competition scoop the market with greater volume at lower prices.

## Penetration

The need for fast sales growth can be akin to riding a wave – miss it and you have missed out. Enough activity can generate word of mouth and/or provide the critical levels of distribution necessary for advertising to be cost effective. One of the key differences between the wine and spirit industry and branded foods has been a propensity for premium priced entry for drinks and penetration strategies for foods. This is partly a difference in the amount of 'heritage' needed to persuade consumers to accept the brand. Heritage is more important for drinks and takes time to build.

Foods, on the other hand, need rapid distribution. To get that retailers need to be assured that heavy advertising is part of the package. Penetration pricing encourages trial.

Most of all it discourages new competitors. If the margins are lower and shelves are full, the gap for a latecomer is less.

## Retaliating first

The micro-computer industry is strewn with examples of the established companies struggling with down-pricing as new competitors invade. Apple had development problems with Mac which delayed the launch and increased the costs. New entrants were forcing down competitive prices at the same time. It was a double whammy. A decreasing price spiral is very hard to stop. Ultimately enough companies go bust or leave the business for profitability to be restored. There is no magic to stopping the spiral; the objective has to be to stop the spiral beginning.

Continuous technical development, as in electronics, is more difficult to manage than known change points such as deregulation, reduction in tariffs or increasing quotas, major new entrants or the expiry of patents.

Especially when there is reason to expect strong, lower-priced competition, the strategy should be to take the hit immediately *before* it becomes necessary. This builds customer and consumer loyalty and makes the competitor's lot more difficult. It is not an easy decision. The short term profits will certainly be lower than the previous plan figure. They may even be lower than they would be, initially, if no action was taken. Nevertheless the likelihood is that the profit decrease will prove less over the medium term than would otherwise be the case.

You will probably not believe it. Quite right; the theory cannot be proved with examples. Every case is different. Any company facing such a situation should recognize it has a major problem on its hands and turn, for once, to quantitative methods. These decisions are rare. Management will not get a second shot; rewinding the video will not play it again. The appropriate degree of sophistication will vary but the need is to play out, or model, the possible repercussions of the alternative strategies. Designing full market simulation models may take more time and money than is available. The basic PC spreadsheet and data packages provide enough software to create simple 'what if' projections within a few hours. All this can do is aid judgement, true, but aiding judgement before critical pricing decisions is the time to do it.

An alternative or additional move is to introduce a price flanking brand in parallel with the one under threat. The purpose of this is simply to keep the competitor busy enough with the flanker to keep the heat away from the breadwinner. So long as the flanker does not lose serious money, you are ahead.

## Grandmother's footsteps

Should pricing be decided by market research, asking customers and consumers how they will react to price alternatives? Save your money. Consumers do not like price increases and they do not necessarily want large decreases either. If market researchers are allowed to ask hypothetical questions, they will get dumb answers. Rational consumers will prefer to pay less for the same quality rather than more but this is not just a matter of rationality. Brands are there to provide consistency. In an age where change is constant, consistency is attractive.

Unless visibility is positively required for some reason, pricing may be a matter of 'Grandmother's Footsteps'. In this game the consumer is Grandmother. The players aim to move by only small steps so that whenever Grandmother turns to look they seem to be standing still. In the original game, anyone caught moving has to go back to the playground wall. In marketing, sales momentum suffers.

There are many techniques for changing prices discreetly without the greater error of misleading customers and consumers. UK banks had a bad press in 1991. One of their mistakes was to vary their charges, already complex and excessive in the eyes of their customers, without adequate notice. Somehow price changes have to slip in above the threshold of awareness but below the threshold where customers or consumers change attitudes, still less behaviour.

One advantage of following the competition is the camouflage they provide. Let them take the heat and then just follow. Such is the privilege of brand leadership. The strategy depends on the brand leader pursuing a progressive pricing policy.

In the 1960s, the Distillers Company (DCL) rarely moved prices at all. Chancellors of the Exchequer did their best to fill the vacuum with duty increases. The strategy was to take advantage of the economies of scale that should have been open to their market share in excess of 50 per cent and squeeze the smaller competitors. Ultimately the competition, primarily Bells in Scotland, took the lead in price and then in share. Bells were canny. They ceased to match discounts slowly but progressively.

They matched prices for one sector (pubs and on premise consumption) whilst appearing to be more valuable where net prices were more obvious: the supermarkets. The DCL policy backfired; they lost both the profits that were open to them, the reputation for quality and brand leadership.

Low profile may be provided by seasonality. Many businesses will raise prices just after the peak trading period where both customers and consumers have had their fill and are in no mood to purchase anyway.

Another window for the invisible price adjuster is just prior to the holiday season when again minds are not so set on the trench warfare of negotiating. Have you ever wondered why actual wars typically begin in August ? Or just before dawn? The return from the annual holiday is the true beginning of the new year. Invigorated, ready for anything, a price change might be just what one needs to set off changed buying patterns. Put up your prices before the holiday; cut them, if you must, after.

Perhaps pricing is more than a children's game of Grand-mothers' Footsteps but the model is closer than that of economic, rational man. It is a game which competitors, customers and consumers all play in ways that can broadly be predicted if time is taken to work it through. Some probabilities can be ascribed to each scenario. Judgement can be assisted. Computers should be increasingly used to simulate the market, competitor responses and answer the 'what if' questions. They will not use the simplistic equations of the past but track customer and consumer responses as they really happen in the market place. In the mean time, paradigm shifts apart, com-panies will not go far astray by walking in Grandmother's Footsteps.

- **MEMO TO FILE**

*Subject:* PRICING

- There can be few marketers in any doubt about the significance of pricing in the marketing mix. Playing Follow-My-Leader is generally a low risk policy. Anything else needs quantitative analysis to support and refine management judgement and intuition.
- Pricing, deals, discounts, special offers must be under control. Every decision maker needs to see and understand the whole picture. If your finance and IT people cannot deliver that today, ask them when they can.
- Control is essential not just for the profit of today or tomorrow but to deal with the increasing power of retailers and the trend towards regionalization/ globalization.
- Pricing needs to follow clear and consistent strategies which are as invisible as possible to competitors, customers and consumers. New launches and repositionings should choose one between the extremes of skimming and penetration. Major new entrants or paradigm shifts should be anticipated with action before the event.
- Until more sophisticated models prove successful for day to day pricing, play a game of Grandmother's Footsteps: move with the herd. Be invisible. Take small steps often: avoid the conspicuous. Otherwise you may force the consumer to wonder why he is buying the brand.
- If you do decide to go for price visibility, use quantitative methods to help you work out all the possible consequences for market share, sales, profits and brand equity. Pricing spirals are easy to start and tough to stop. Someone is going to go bust and it might be you.

# P

# 22. Public relations

**ISSUES:**

1. Making friends with the media.
2. Time versus money.
3. Events that fit.

## 1. MAKING FRIENDS WITH THE MEDIA

Why spend more on advertising when editorial space is available free of charge? Once word of mouth starts to work for (or against) your brand, nothing else is more powerful. Moet et Chandon powered their domination of champagne in Europe through public relations, with only rare excursions into advertising.

When public relations works right, nothing else can match it. For most brands, most of the time, it is a side show.

The essence of PR is the recognition that journalists have space to fill with news, not advertising. Journalists want exclusivity and believe that whatever marketers tell them is puffery. When hard news has to be circulated fast and visibly, such as when announcing an acquisition, a press release is both necessary and effective. But in the more subtle world of trying to gain free space for marketing messages, press releases can be discounted. If it is not exclusive, forget it.

Much of the best PR, for this reason, is happenstance. Organized companies are able to maximize advantage from such serendipity. The USA wine and spirit industry, which has been assailed by anti-alcohol propaganda, has refrained from singing the praises of its products. Sales slipped sharply between 1989 and 1991. Then the programme *60 Minutes*, watched by over 20 million, broadcast the 'French paradox' which stated that the high fat content of the French diet was not the killer American doctors thought it should be. Investigative research concluded that their intake of red wine provided a prophylactic. American sales of Californian Cabernet Sauvignon jumped 45 per cent, sliding to a steady 25 per cent increase after two months. The wine makers did their best to let the 200 million other Americans who missed the programme know all about it.

The journalist's interest in digging for exclusive stories lies at the heart of the mixed relationship between marketers and the media. Both should be on the same side; consumers really are interested in the brands they buy. Tales of Persil in Taiwan are no more vacuous than stories of media personalities holidaying in Casablanca. In both cases, the journalist has to convince the reader that he or she is on the inside: here is what is actually going on behind the scenes.

The same factors can work in advertising. People want to know about the Gold Blend couple in the long running TV commercials romance. When the fictitious J. R. Hartley used Yellow Pages to trace a copy of his book out of print on fly fishing, people started going into bookshops and asking for it. Soon a publisher provided it. Nature imitated advertising.

The marketer is faced with a simple choice: make friends with media people, or forget about PR. The public relations agency will dress matters up in swirling professionalism; pay no attention. PR specialists play an important role, but journalists want to speak directly with the marketer or CEO. They want facts, eloquence and enthusiasm. Recognize the common interests with journalists or expect little free space.

Mutual trust begins with acceptance that 'off the record'

means what it says. If it is not actually said, then anything goes. The vast majority of journalists respect the convention meticulously, but only if the magic words are spoken. Within a relationship (marketing, once again, is the business of managing relationships), discreet bargaining is possible. The journalist wants a usable story; the marketer wants the brand name spelt right. In one sense the marketer does not care what is said so long as the story fits the heritage of the brand.

Moet et Chandon spent hours chasing winning occasions, especially motor racing, with free magnums. These Magna Go-carters were photo opportunities, never mind the rationale. The story was irrelevant; the picture communicated celebration and success.

## Crisis management

The organization necessary to prepare for unexpected good news works equally well for bad. Plenty has been written about crisis management but it all adds up to preparedness. Any top PR operation, inside or out, maintains high level relationships with media and top management, drills them in handling awkward situations and knows where to find them at any time. More than one CEO's spouse has had to phone the PR department to locate her other half.

There are three levels of response. Being unprepared, responding adequately and turning it into an opportunity to promote the company. The DCL handled thalidomide as badly as it could be done. They were dragged from admission to concession grudgingly from year to year. Perrier handled their benzene crisis adequately in that they were seen to be prompt and decisive. British Midland turned their motorway crash disaster into an opportunity through the immediacy and compassion shown by their chief executive. Both the awareness of and attitudes to British Midland were greater after the event.

## 2. TIME VERSUS MONEY

Few brands have the advantages of Moet, but the potential for

PR in the marketing mix is worth assessing. The subtleties of the vehicle justify a professional review. To have a specialist agency pitch for the business is, like the whole of PR, light on money but heavy on time. Every column inch secured by Moet was free but the amount of time invested by their staff to achieve that publicity was daunting. Just to brief an agency to the point where they can pitch will burn hours away.

A pitch will presumably tell you that PR is needed. The interesting issues relate to how, what and who:

- How to get you messages across
- What they should be
- Who, i.e. which journalists or media, will find your messages newsworthy enough to give them space

A good agency will be tough; it is part of their job to make marketers see messages from the journalist's point of view. Whether the agency gets the business or not, it should become clear what PR can do for the brands in question.

Balancing the time and money costs against likely benefits, deciding on outside or internal PR help or neither or both, will all come down to judgement. PR benefits are largely unmeasurable. The key decision is whether PR becomes an important part of the mix. If it does not, then some fairly basic training on do's and don'ts will equip a few people with all they need to get some messages out and deal with incoming questions or crises.

If PR is a serious lever, then it needs professional handling both for objectivity and time reasons.  It looks easy, and some CEOs have natural gifts for it. Even so, a company needs something better than a mirror to describe the way it looks. Moreover the business of getting close enough to journalists for mutual partnership will take more from the diary than any CEO should have to spare.

## 3.   EVENTS THAT FIT

Do you suspect a company announcing a new golf sponsorship of having a CEO who plays golf? That certainly used to be true.

It may still be, but sensitivity now surrounds such use of corporate power to conceal the extent.

Let us assume you have decided to make PR a major part of your agency programme and are reviewing a short list of PR professionals. When they get to specific proposals, expect to hear about this great 'event' which will carry the brand name, interest the media, be a hospitality opportunity for your best customers and introduce you to famous and/or beautiful people.

Events can be just a Pavlovian PR response. They are tangible, finite and chargeable. Food and drink flows. PR people barely need to eat at home; they must have the lowest Sainsbury's bills of any in their socio-economic group. Events are portable too: if one client turns this great idea down, it just goes back in the tool bag for the next.

Bright creative events are indeed valuable but they are not essential. They deserve all the cynicism they get. Apart from the usual cost/benefit issues, the key questions are the same as for advertising: does the event reinforce the brand positioning? What will it do for awareness and attitudes? How long will it take to be effective? Some of the best events run for 25 years before the full value shows up. What are you getting into?

CEOs are entitled to some perks. If she really hates boxing then, whatever the marketing rationale, she is not going to sponsor boxing. At the same time the selection of an event is likely to be a long-term decision, longer than any CEO should expect to remain in office. Taking that long view, create events to serve your brand. The Hennessy Cognac Gold Cup is 'the Hennessy': it was created for the brand. The Ever Ready Derby is still 'the Derby'.

Whilst the 'have event, will travel' approach is to to be ridiculed, matching the event to the purpose is another matter. I do not wish to insult bank managers (especially mine) or cricket lovers by suggesting either could be boring but consider the perfect positioning of NatWest Bank sponsoring cricket. Where else could bankers have the uninterrupted attention of their major customers for hours at a time? If the event truly fits the brand positioning, then the benefits can build and build.

- **MEMO TO FILE**

*Subject:* PUBLIC RELATIONS

- Assess if PR rates a serious part of the brand's marketing programme. If it does use the time and objectivity of professionals.

- Make friends with a few, carefully selected, media people with shared interests.

- Be ruthless in the choice of events. Create new ones that fit.

$$\boxed{P}$$

# 23.   Promotions, coupons and giveaways

**ISSUES:**

1. Price promotions are a waste of money, yet they continue. Reasons for and against.
2. Sampling, on the other hand, is vital.
3. Quantity discounts strengthen customer relationships, within limits.
4. Use non-price promotions as "advertising". Reinforce positioning.
5. Coupons are cheapening.

## 1.   PRICE PROMOTIONS – A WASTE OF TIME?

Most marketers regard price promotions as a waste of money yet, most of them still run price promotions. Why? Trying to explain marketing is tough enough without having to explain marketers.

Price promotions are temporary money off for the customer and/or consumer, or, alternatively, an extra amount of the product free of charge. After advertising, promotions are the most conspicuous and frequent form of demand stimulation marketing. Success depends on context, execution and timing.

Even within those three caveats, marketing activity cannot be divided into good and bad. Such generalizations would be unprofessional.

Nevertheless: *Price promotions are bad.* They are fun to start and the devil to stop. Serious marketers wish they had never started. Price promotions are no more, and no less, addictive than cocaine.

In the six months to March 1992, a number of leading companies in the USA announced that they would terminate price promotions and bring in an 'every-day low price'. Procter & Gamble, Kraft and Alpo (a brand leader for dog food) were three of them. It was a brave move which may or may not succeed. Price promotions can be distinguished from other techniques such as sampling new consumers (good), quantity discounts (good if rational), non-price promotions (good if they reinforce the brand's positioning) and coupons. Coupons are those tacky bits of paper you send off or redeem with the check-out for money off the next purchase or suchlike. They have the advantage over general price promotions in that they segment the market. In other words, those who want a lower price, cash them. Those who cannot be bothered do not. It is efficient only to offer discount to those who insist; otherwise, coupons are just as bad as general price promotions.

Promotions are a complex area and this brief introduction needs to cut a few corners for the sake of clarity. We will look at price promotions first because that is where the money has been going.

Within the price promotional, or primevil (sic), swamp, five motivations can be discerned:

- *Whoever begins a new cycle has a short term advantage.* Customers take more product, more facings are available on shelf, market share expands. Some of the gains may be permanent. It is important to note the cyclical nature. Once everyone stops in the name of insanity, there is a lull. Then it starts again.
- *Retailers love them.* They make the retailer competitive against his competitor, the store becomes lively, and the

increase in sales of the promoted brand will more than offset losses from others. His sales and profits will increase both immediately and long-term as customers attracted by deals return. Only part of the promotional money from the brand owner will be passed on to the consumer; the balance will go straight into the retailer's own pocket. We will see why in a moment.

- *The sales force loves them.* With a regular calendar of promotions, there is always something new to discuss, visible displays to achieve and largesse to dispense.

- *Short termism.* The brand manager has targets to make by a fixed date. Loading the dealers moves profit from next period into the current one. In some organizations, failing to meet this year's target means you will not be around for the next one.

- *The competition is promoting.* Brands that do not compete have a way of disappearing from shelves. Once the cycle has begun, it is difficult not at least to match what others are offering. If your company has established a pattern of such offers, how do you explain to the customer why you are stopping? Sewing up a hole in the pocket is great for everyone, except the person picking up the coins.

You will have noticed that the consumer does not appear on this list. Surely money off purchases is what the consumer wants? Marketing is serving consumer needs and promotions are just that. Some go further and see marketing as a 3D activity: display, discount and dominate. Particularly in a recession, this notion has its attractions. Creating bustle in the stores at least contributes cash flow; and the importance of winter and summer sales to retailers has long been established. The semi-continuous sales now available many be expensive, but bustle provides the opportunity for hustle. When you walk into a marketplace, are you attracted by the busy stall or the unattended one?

Price promotions run by retailers from their own resources are at once good and important both for them and the consumer. A market philosophy depends on individuals freely deciding how their money should be used. Why then the hostility to those promotions being funded by brand owners?

It comes down to a recognition of roles. Retailers do not add value to a brand (there are exceptions which we will ignore). Their role is to move stock quickly and efficiently to the consumer. To some extent they create demand, but they owe no allegiance to any particular brand.

The brand owner, however, has to differentiate that brand from competitors, provide reasons to buy and, very likely, create demand for the category as a whole. Building a brand is expensive. Any funds for the retailer's role are taken from brand building. The loss of brand equity may be slow to appear. The diversion from long-term brand building to short-term volume gains can be justified when the net effect is positive. The evidence is otherwise. Price promotions do not build brands.

The area is contentious. Some brand owners argue that the growth of power in the hands of a few retailers will ultimately strangle new brand development and competition. What seems providential for consumers in the short term may be less attractive later.

Brand owners have acquired a powerful weapon in the recovery of promotional funds: electronic point-of-sale tills. Until point-of-sale data could be captured, it was not possible to identify the price at which brands were sold. Retailers, or Neilsen or other agencies, would establish sales by counting stock and adjusting purchases by the stock differences from period to period. Since the sales turnover was known by product category, some allowance could be made for 'shrinkage', that element of stock that disappears through breakages, pilferage, shoplifting or inexplicable reasons.

Now electronic systems allow the brand owner to compare the amount of product discounted *to* the retailer with the amount of product discounted *by* the retailer. Estimates vary, but it appears that the consumer is receiving only 25 to 50 per cent of the funding provided by the brand owner. At the very least, brand owners will seek to tie their offers more closely with retailers' offers. Brand owners can now regain some control over their products.

In an age of retailer power, such tightening will not be easy. Today retailers demand and obtain stocking, or 'slotting' or listing, fees for adding a new line from a supplier, and then the same again for taking it off the computer when sales decline. Once brand owners start to use point of sale data to reduce retailer benefits, will they still get the data?

Two more factors disturb brand marketers:

- A brand is a brand because it supplies consistency to the consumer. Confidence is a key ingredient. What effect does constantly changing price have on the consumer? Is loyalty impacted? If brands A and B are on offer on alternate weeks, does that prompt consumers to alternate between A and B and ultimately move to the cheapest? In the UK, retailer own brand groceries have increased steadily to 30 per cent of the market.
- There is evidence that discounting reduces the perception of quality. As quality is in the eye of the consumer, one can say that price promotions actually reduce quality. That will damage any brand that includes quality in its positioning.

How can one kick the price promotion addiction? The first step is to recognize that it is bad. The second is to recognize that only very strong companies can step alone out of the competitive spiral. Collusion to stop price promotions is illegal in most western countries. Some will think that illegality is reason enough not to collude; others will be deterred by the difficulty of enforcing illegitimate deals. What happens much more frequently is an intensive campaign of competitive signalling. Competitive signalling can take many forms. One company after another draws attention to the negative attributes of excessive price promotions, very possibly in the trade press, or academics write sponsored papers. The signs of this activity were apparent in 1991.

Once the climate is adjusted, small moves can be made by small players or bigger moves by the larger ones. If they are followed, the problem is solved, for the moment.

## Value Promotions

'Value promotions' are additional product in place of, or sometimes in addition to, lower prices. They have the following advantages over price promotions:

- *Consumers like them.* 10 per cent more coffee in a pack is more tangible than a 10 per cent discount from a price they do not remember and may not believe.
- *Because the packs are different they track through the distributive chain.* The consumer gets what the retailer gets.
- *The cost to the brand owner is less* especially when, as in a recession, he has spare product in his inventories.

Production like them less (special packaging) though they can off-load surplus.

Value promotions have gained in favour over price promotions of which they are a less virulent form.

## 2. SAMPLING NEW CONSUMERS

Not only new brands need new consumers; every brand needs them to stay alive. Consumers, on the other hand, are not desperate for new brands. A supermarket already carries thousands of lines, far more than any one consumer will ever need. Progressively greater varieties of retailer offer still more brands.

Sampling is as good as price promotion is bad. If sampling is contingent on lower pricing, think about it.

Most promotional activity associated with going to trial can be quantified. Demonstrators can sample the brand to consumers in store. Samples or vouchers or coupons can be direct mailed. There are fairs, on-street sampling, products given away with established brands, gifts in hotel rooms or at charity functions. The list is endless. They can all be tried on a small scale; the costs and conversion rates can be measured.

What cannot be measured is the way the sampling relates to the brand's positioning. To be offered a new variety of cheddar cheese by a demonstrator in a supermarket is one thing. But what about caviar?

The practice of marketing may be all the better for being inconsistent; it may baffle the competition. Inconsistency on a single brand, however, loses the consumer.

## 3. QUANTITY DISCOUNTS

On the surface, quantity discounts have the same money-off characteristics as price promotions. Again, most of the benefit will stay with the retailer. By bunching purchases, the retailer can obtain the same temporary advantages. The differences are significant:

- Quantity discounts are year round. The retailer may use them to fund promotions, but they do not encourage rapid price changes.
- They can be structured to smooth product flow and minimize costs for the supplier. If an order costs £100 to process and deliver, irrespective of the size of the order, it may make sense to discount over £100 on the larger quantities. The sales manager will have some complex arithmetic to show that the maximum allowance should be £200, or double any other number you think of. This is not only an incentive to move the order quantity from the customer's optimal point to the supplier's, it is an important difference from price promotions. Those introduce inefficient peaks and troughs into the supply logistics, whereas quantity discounts are designed to iron them out.
- By taking groups of products together, many permutations can be achieved to persuade the buyer to take more of the items he wants less. This is a fine area for computer analysis.
- Most importantly, quantity discounts encourage the retailer to consolidate his buying with the fewest suppliers. The reason the sales manager gives to justify the higher discounts will be to exclude competitors.
- Some legislation frowns on discounting policies which discriminate between customers except for quantity purposes. Quantity discounts may be one of the few ways of legal

discrimination. Within careful choice of break points and assortments, profits can be maximized.

The extent to which these factors affect customer loyalty varies massively. For many companies, quantity discounts will remain an important part of the marketing mix. Once again, consistency is a key ingredient, but discounts should be reviewed annually at the same time as any monthly or yearly rebate scheme. Similar considerations apply to arrangements such as loyalty bonuses based on the share of business a customer gives any one supplier. The mathematical complexities and the money involved well justify testing options through a small PC based model.

## 4. NON-PRICE PROMOTIONS

There are no firm figures of non-price promotion (NPP) expenditure to the UK, but in 1987 it was thought to be about 25 per cent of display advertising expenditure, or in other words, £1,000M.

In reality NPP may include some price ingredients. NPPs are in effect "advertisements". Their function is to convey the brand's positioning and reasons to buy through different media from conventional advertising. At least, consistency is the theory. In practice, a poor NPP well executed will still beat a consistent NPP badly done.

Besides consistency what are we looking for? Relevancy, stand-out, topicality, fashion, originality and adding brand values. Relevancy is how well the promotion supports the product; stand-out secures attention; topicality gets the day (Mother's Day, for example) right and also the year. The purpose of all those characteristics is to add value to the brand. Price and value promotions, on the other hand, subtract value.

NPPs should be fun. Each is an opportunity for the brand and its consumers to share common values in an extended way. Branded t-shirts, match boxes, umbrellas, diaries, ties, playing cards and pens have been around for fifty years. Ashtrays have lost a little glitz and no doubt other promotional media will come and go. But the fun is in the medium, or in what is done with it.

## 5. COUPONS

Coupons come last because that is where they belong. In the UK 8,110,000,000 coupons were distributed in 1991, an increase of 60 per cent on 1990. They are the UK's most widely used promotional tools but Brussels dislikes them.

Coupons distributed in 1991 were more than double those in 1984 but redemptions increased only 65 per cent. One might imagine that recession would encourage redemption but the *percentage* redeemed has almost halved from just over 10 per cent to just over 5 per cent.

Coupons have their advantages. They can be valuable for trial, and before that god, all fall down. They legally discriminate between consumers in a similar way that quantity discounts discriminate between trade purchasers. In economic terms, the supplier maximizes his profit if each buyer pays her highest acceptable price and that is always more than the supplier's cost.

Coupons are expensive to administer and wasteful. At least 25 per cent are 'misredeemed' (i.e. cashed without meeting the conditions). That costs the UK coupon industry £28m a year. Jolly good thing too. They disfigure packaging and newsprint. Is this prejudice? One man's prejudice is another's experience.

As proved the case with wines and spirits in the USA, coupons in the UK seem to be overheating and burning out.

## CONCLUSION

Promotions cover a wide field of ingenuity. Marketers would do well to reduce the concentration on price and focus on sizzling activities which add value. Promotions can be seen as advertising in another medium but there is more flexibility. Marketers who would be embarrassed to copy advertising think little of borrowing promotions from other categories and territories. Promotions are susceptible to testing and quantitative assessment. Expect to be shocked by the lack of thoroughness in testing and performance measurement.

Promotions are the second largest part of the classic marketing mix. Well handled, they will build brands at the same time as throwing off important short term profits.

- **MEMO TO FILE**

*Subject:* PROMOTIONS, COUPONS AND GIVEAWAYS

- Work out what price promotions are costing versus the profit gained. Will competition make that worse or better in future? If you do not like the answer, quit complaining about retailer power. Get even. Use your money to build your own brands, not those of the customers. It may be time for some competitive signalling.

- Do not throw out the pearl of consumer trial with the oyster of promotion. How else are you going to increase business?

- Quantity discounts have a valuable place in securing customer loyalty and economic order sizes. It can be a small but expensive step from there to using quantity discounts as price promotions. Resist it.

- Non-price promotions can be a creative form of advertising through different media. Treat them that way. The medium reinforcing the message is a double win.

- Coupons are cheap. They are useful for gaining trial and price segmenting consumers. Premium brands would be wise to avoid them. In the UK they may be burning out.

- Check out the professionalism not only of the promotions but how they are tested and how well performance is measured against expectations. Without this feedback, learning will be reduced.

## P

# 24.  Personal selling

**ISSUES:**

1. Role of personal selling within the marketing mix.
2. Visiting costs fifty times a phone call. Value from step by step, feedback, competitive intelligence.
3. Managing relationships is a personal business. Trade marketing. Managing the sales force.
4. Selling as partnership.

Pity the poor customer. Ever since Tom Peters told companies to get closer to their customers, personal fresheners have sky-rocketed. And not just sales. One of the holes in the ozone layer has had to be named after him.

Personal selling may have been the poor relation of advertising when it was all image building. Today there are fewer sales people carrying that title but the importance of the function has re-emerged.

## 1.   WHAT IS THE ROLE OF THE SALES EXECUTIVE?

Personal selling was the earliest form of marketing and will be the last for a simple reason: no business can log a profit until it makes a sale. Whoever does it and however it is done, only a sale can trigger the profit scorecard. That should make the sales person the corporate hero. It rarely does.

A number of business thinkers have now reversed the traditional pyramid hierarchy to put the salesforce at the top:

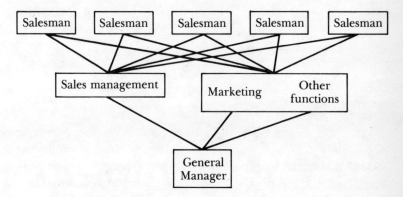

Note: So far as the sales force are concerned, marketing and other functions are only in support.

*Figure 15    Sales force as vanguard*

This is a step in the right direction, but it implies a large number of sales people in proportion to the rest of the business. This is infrequent. Perhaps it is better to consider the single sales person as the spear point with the rest of the business supporting that role. In an industrial or business-to-business marketing company, that model positions the sales person correctly. The consumer marketing model is more complex.

That the triangle shape in figure 16 is also the Greek sign for delta, now used in business to mean change, is a useful reminder that this relationship should be dynamic. The sales river doesn't stand still, and the effect on the customer is constantly changing.

Whether in consumer or business marketing, the sales force should be given more recognition and support. They are the flag bearers. Their commitment, enthusiasm, passion, determination translate directly into corporate success. There is no

*Figure 16    Salesman as arrowhead*

substitute.

Have you ever come across a business where someone would not draw you to one side and explain confidentially that one should ignore the externals, 'this is really a people business'? Is there any other kind? The fundamental seller/buyer transaction is fuelled not just by mechanistic economic factors but by personal trust and beliefs. And who, may I ask, will inspire these human qualities if it is not the sales force? In this context the 'sales force' refers to everyone involved in selling to customers, whatever their title.

Products move through the distribution chain both in response to consumer pull and to supplier push, i.e. personal selling. One may be more effective than the other. The balance may shift with the economic climate, but both are needed for consumer brand marketing. In business-to-business or indust- rial marketing, there is little 'pull'; personal selling forms the main 'push'.

Network marketing, such as Amway, Tupperware and, more recently, air fresheners and water purifiers, which depends largely on personal selling though word-of-mouth, also helps creates some degree of consumer pull. Not surprisingly, the recession has seen some increase in door-to-door selling.

To the marketing manager, personal selling is more than just an element of the marketing mix to be costed against advertising or PR or promotions, it is an organic part of the business fuelling not only customer relationships but stimulating the marketing function with feedback from the market.

## 2.  THE COSTS OF SELLING

Attention to personal selling focuses partly on how to maximize the value from this specialist form of marketing and partly on cost. Taking salary, bonuses, car, expenses and on-costs together a junior sales person may cost £50,000 a year. A specialist industrial sales person may cost twice that. A junior making 1,800 customer calls a year or a specialist making 1,000 gives a cost per call ranging from £30 to £100. Small wonder companies have cut numbers back and looked for lower cost alternatives.

Personal selling here includes two of the most popular lower cost variants: telephone sales (now called, misleadingly, telemarketing) and brokers. The techniques for telesales differ from those of personal visits more than was at first thought. Information systems support, for example, is more critical. The database support needed for telesales is not far different from that required for other forms of direct marketing such as mail. With about ten times the daily calling capacity and half the base cost structure, the cost per call is nearer £2 than £30. (All figures in 1990 money). Development of such databases is growing in significance. They offer substantial competitive advantages as well as contemporary values.

Brokers offer a shared sales service to a number of suppliers. If the supplier has a small portfolio, brokers provide critical mass and cost/efficiency. The broker will develop specialist sales and management skills with, consequentially, greater productivity. A final attraction of brokers is that they are compensated on a commission basis. Arrangements vary but tying selling costs tightly to sales is valuable to many businesses, especially to those just starting up.

Should the brand marketer develop the same skills as brokers? Some do. The Mars group, for example, has an outstanding record for training and management of sales people. But to some the sales force is almost taken for granted. The most traditional, in a sense, of company functions and making only rare appearance in headquarters the sales force's greatest visibility in these companies is in the profit and loss account.

Increasing costs and retailer power together with declining margins have forced a re-examination. No longer do retailers want store visits from sales people; some will not accept them. They want lower prices, but want also to control their own supply of product and information to branches. As the big retailers increase their share of market so the size of the sales force diminishes, but their importance does not. The key account sales person handling that retailer might have the power to make or break the marketer.

**MARKETER**                                    **RETAILER**

*Figure 17    Complex sales relationships*

This has led to complex vertical sales structures where the marketer sells to the retailer at several different levels, e.g. regionally, to central buyers and to the buying director. The key account sales person's relationship with the buyer is thus flanked by the regional sales manager's relationship with the customer's regional management and the sales director's relationship with her opposite number. In this respect consumer brand marketing has moved closer to industrial marketing, where these complex multi-link relationships have long been the norm.

## 3. MANAGING RELATIONSHIPS IS A PERSONAL BUSINESS

That convergence is underlined by the creation of 'trade' or 'customer' marketing departments. Large consumer marketing companies in both Europe and the USA have recognized that the power of large retailers, the complexity of promotions and relationships are demanding specialist attention within marketing. The product manager is ultimately concerned with the consumer, and may not be giving the customer enough attention. Furthermore, there may be as many product managers as brands. That is fine from a consumer viewpoint but the customer expects the supplier's activities to be coordinated, if not tailored, especially for him.

A trade marketing department has the responsibility of bringing promotions, sales presentations and information together, both brand by brand and in total, for the customer with his attitudes in mind. While it is then up to the sales person to manage the ensuing relationship, performance can be hugely increased by professional pre-packaging of the sales effort.

Improved performance can be measured not just in sales turnover, better mix and margins, but in improved control over price promotions and the contributions paid over by brand marketers.

There are good reasons for the division any company makes between the promotional funds in the marketing department budget and the discounts and allowances that come from sales or from the gross margin. From the sales person's point of view, giving money from the marketing budget will look better than giving it from his own. The brand or product manager may also prefer this if she is getting what she wants. Furthermore, the funding in the marketing budget may be split with an overseas supplier.

A large consumer goods company would be well advised to consider a trade marketing department and to bonus both them and sales on the basis that there is no featherbedding by marketing. Whatever the source of promotional funding or price adjustments, the sales function picks up the tab. How internal accounting can be structured to achieve this will be a difficulty, but it is worth putting the accountability of sales onto the same basis as the organization as a whole.

A number of computer packages now offer systems to measure account profitability and, as a by-product, the profitability of the sales person responsible for those accounts. There are many ways to reduce the cost of promotions, but three basic steps are:

1. Make the sales person profit-responsible so that his goals are consistent with those of the business as a whole.
2. Ensure the sales person has all the information relevant to that account. Now that electronic point of sale (EPOS) data can match promotions granted to consumers with those given to retailers, the sales person has high quality information to help fine tune terms. Sales people of the future will need facts from databases, not exhortation and stories.
3. Raise productivity by providing specialist support through trade marketing. Measure performance of this support too.

The management of a sales force is subject to cultural norms. Brits expect to be independent, Germans to be regimented, Italians to be creative, French to be intellectual, South Africans to think they are training for rugby. Feel free to apply your own stereotypes. A universal feature, however, is the regular sales conference. Budgets may influence the frequency and extravagance of these, but the key point is that the management does at least try to tell the sales force how much it loves them.

The value of a sales conference cannot be measured, nor should it be skimped. It is a high point of inspiring passion and commitment. Every day cannot be a sales conference but a lot can be done to maintain those attitudes through the year.

'Closer to the customer' is a modern cliché but the appeal is real: if you are close enough to feel how he feels, you are also that much closer to his wallet. But the concept fails to take account of the sales person who is already close to the customer. Why not get closer to the sales force?

## 4. SELLING AS PARTNERSHIP

Understanding one's business from the outside in, from the consumer's point of view and also the customer's, is basic to marketing; that is what a market orientation means. It also underlies the whole concept and measurement of quality. One is in partnership with the customer; the role is not adversarial. Together, marketer and customer help the consumer buy more.

There is evidence that a partnership relationship within a distribution channel between supplier and the outlets is more profitable for both sides than parochial maximization of profitability. Some thinkers go further and claim that lower consumer prices will also result. That seems doubtful; and there are also legal restraints on retail price agreements. Nevertheless, the general principle that cooperation is more profitable than competition remains true.

For this reason companies may now regard their sales personnel more as consultants assisting customers to realize their profit opportunities. Any marketing trend creates a counter-trend as companies look for points of difference. Moving further and further into the customer's business as consultants has benefits of involvement and understanding, but problems of cost and distraction. The counter-trend is to revert to the basics where the supplier is hammering away at the front door to get volume and market share.

Procter & Gamble USA seem to be moving back to this foot in the jaw routine. Their strong market share and the consumer 'pull' created by their brands and weight of advertising are such that this strategy is rational for them.

Within selling there are wide variations from foot-in-the-door to consultative, short-term (transactional) to long term relationships, individual to team, volume orientation to profit responsibility. The list does not stop there. The John Lewis organization, for example, calls its sales people 'partners' and treats with them in exactly that way. In aggregate these characteristics make up the company's 'style' of customer relationships. Even if the perfect balance can be found, style will need to change over time both to refresh and stimulate the team and to provide competitive advantage.

It is good to review the size, balance and composition of the sales effort every year or so, but why stop there? Consider the need for a sales force in-house. How important is maximizing outward push and inward market feedback? The balance with other parts of the marketing mix, and style of selling (consultative, partnership, aggressive) also need fundamental consideration every now and then. How does three yearly sound to you? Marketing is ultimately the managing of relationships. Nowhere is this more visible than in personal selling.

- **MEMO TO FILE**

*Subject:* PERSONAL SELLING

- Are the sales force the heroes of the business? Do they have the passion, commitment, recognition and support they need? They should believe they are the most important people in your business and they probably are.

- Marketing is about managing relationships. They begin and end with the customer relationship. What training, information and support will improve those relationships? What is done at the centre that could be better done in the field? Would specialist trade marketing help or just add to overhead?

- Personal selling may be the most expensive component in the marketing mix. Optimize the size of the sales force and rebalance territories or responsibilities annually. Review selling style then.

- Compromise quantity but not quality. Better to provide more than they can handle. Make each sales person profit responsible. Then their goals synchronize with those of the business as a whole.

# 25. Pragmatic planning

**ISSUES:**

1. Is strategic planning a contradiction in terms?
2. Why bother with planning at all?
3. Planning headlines.
4. Harnessing finance and systems support.

## 1. STRATEGIC PLANNING

Some form of professional annual plan is so basic to marketing that it must surely be universal practice? In the loosest sense it is: marketing actions are not taken without some prior thought, if only a millisecond before. In the formal sense, however, only about 7 per cent of medium/large UK marketing companies produce 'plans', defined here to contain at least analysis, strategy, actions (who is going to do what and when) and a budget. This rough estimate was taken from a much more precise study by Laura Cousins. On the other hand, 60 per cent have some kind of planning process. Are the text book imperatives on planning right or should we accept what companies actually do?

In addition to the annual plan, larger companies expect

longer term or strategic plans. The conventional text book wisdom is to define objectives, then strategy, tactics and increasingly lower levels of detail until the specific actions are identified. In this 'cascade' model, each flows logically from the other. It is rational, sensible and wrong. Yet this top down process has become ingrained in western thinking. Oriental approaches to strategy are more sophisticated and are now being adopted more widely. Sun Tzu wrote perhaps the definitive work over 2,000 years ago called *The Art of War* (also translated as the *Art of Strategy*). In essence he proposes that overall objectives and direction are made clear together with the necessary training to allow actions to be flexibly decided only when they need to be and in the light of prevailing circumstances. In modern language, such training and local action is equivalent to corporate learning and empowerment.

For most companies, strategy is what you discover you were doing after you have been successful. Luck forms a part. So do your responses to unforecast events. Strategy is fine if it gives a consistent orientation to deal with the unexpected. What is daft is the cascading of plans from the general to the specific, the sequential branching of decision making before there is any need to make those decisions.

Modern strategy writers, such as Henry Mintzberg, have incorporated this thinking into defining the strategic thrust and leaving the detail to be worked out later. The latest decision is likely to be the best. Anticipation dissipates time and resources. Planning productivity depends on knowing when to start planning and when to stop. Start later and stop sooner than you think.

Even in a game without luck (or 'positive stochastic outcomes'), the analytic decision tree approach where each option is followed through all its logical possibilities has been abandoned. Humans cannot do it and nor can computers. What they use is a predetermined pattern of play which gives a general shape but is flexible enough to respond to unexpected moves by the opponent. Some call this strategy. Marketing people call it positioning.

Many of the largest companies, such as Shell and General Electric, have long abandoned long term detailed planning on the cascade model. Shell has used 'scenarios' since the 1970s so that management can try out responses to alternative possible future situations. General Electric has switched its efforts from elaborate planning systems to developing its managers internationally. By showing them different ways of doing things in other countries, they are being trained in the Sun Tzu sense. What they have in common is the determination of corporate strategy in broad terms. This requires the specification of the 'vision' of what the company is trying to become, the culture and the principles which should guide the management responses to individual problems and opportunities. The theory is that lower level managers can then be empowered to make decisions without intrusive planning and controls.

Planning should have less to do with writing it down than agreeing internally what is going to happen. Entrepreneurial companies, whether still led by the founder or with a dominant chief executive, may not have any planning process at all. The chief executive makes it up as he goes along. That was how he got where he is. The formula is more likely to continue to be successful than not in any given year but will ultimately be replaced. Either the business will fail or the chief executive will be replaced. The incoming CEO, whether from inside or out, will need a planning process of some kind if only to produce clarity and consensus.

## WHY BOTHER WITH PLANNING AT ALL?

There is nothing magic about planning. It is only second best to the flair of a successful entrepreneur. That said, professional planning is still well ahead of the alternatives. Why so? Four reasons:

1. *Planning internalizes corporate learning.* The cycle is fundamental to any learning activity though it appears in different forms and language. For the owner/entrepreneur there is no need to write this down. Professional managers come and go. The latest annual plan should be the reference manual for a new manager. A good plan will never match the width of

collective experience of her new colleagues but nothing else will be so clear or so precise.

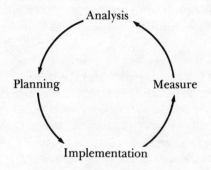

*Figure 18   The planning cycle*

2. *Planning can promote creativity and innovation.* This is more of a 'should' than a 'will'. If the corporate culture is static, then the annual plan may be little more than the previous year's with the dates changed. Comparing the two years' plans will make the extent of development, or the lack of it, obvious. If the previous effort is still firing on all cylinders, then indeed it should be continued. More generally, each year throws up areas for improvement. In some companies, however, planning has provided more opportunities to be destructive of new thinking, motivation or flexibility. These and lack of resources for planning are typical reasons why planning does not take place.

3. *Planning should require participation.* A principle function of marketing is to link together the activities of the different functions, to coordinate the efforts of buying, production, operations and sales behind the brand or whatever unit is used for planning purposes. To prepare an initial draft the marketing manager may well need to find a quiet spot and wrap wet towel around fevered brow. Thereafter planning should be an interactive process. A plan is no more than the minutes of the meetings which agreed strategy, actions and budgets. The lessons from prior years and analysis which led

to the agreement should be documented for future learning but are not critical to what has to be done. Participation should include outside agencies (eg advertising) where their commitment is required to the final conclusions.

4. *Planning delivers commitment.* Unless those whose actions are required feel some 'ownership' of the plan, its implementation will be less effective. In the entrepreneurial model, 'ownership' may be replaced by discipline or even fear. The clarity of a good plan will assist implementation. Budgets and responsibilities should be unequivocal. Battling a draft plan to and fro should produce both innovation, realism and commitment but only if enough time is given by participants to the process.

If plans give these advantages, why do 93 per cent of UK marketing companies not bother with a formal plan as defined here? Mainly because it is a chore. Once agreement is reached, those concerned are clear about it, especially in smaller companies. A written plan may simply be filed and not seen again. Others recall plans from textbooks as being onerous. Plans can be cumbersome; the detail is largely irrelevant or well known to everyone in the business.

To work laboriously down from environment through competition to strategy, policies, tactics and actions can be a tedious way to get into what you were going to do anyway. Each step of the cascade purports to maximize the net present value of future profits. Can you really do that? The textbook plan is built up from blank paper as if nothing existed before. In reality, managers are incrementalists. There is a strict limit to the amount that next year's plan can differ from this. When the current plan is working well, there is good reason to continue.

If the physical process of preparing a plan is laborious, then many of the benefits will be driven out by the effort involved. The objective switches from building the brand to getting the plan done.

## 3. PLAN HEADLINES

A professional marketer should have a written plan but it should be short and tightly focused. The first stage is to agree a skeleton format. Libertarians will object that creativity will be driven out by a planning process that requires boxes to be filled in. Every brand and every year is different. Filling boxes will cause irrelevant detail to be included. Piffle! Format free planning makes as much sense as leaving education to ten year olds to figure out for themselves. Planning is learning. Senior management have an obligation to provide the framework for the kind of analysis they expect to be done. Detail should certainly be added only where relevant. If there will be no media spend, then there need be no media policy.

Plans have many uses. Some plans used to gain approval for spending are rather less than specific, for example. A plan may be a political campaign document. Dignifying these practices as 'internal marketing' gives marketing a bad name. Let us assume that the plan is the real one.

The provision of some guideline headings is with trepidation. Despite the comments above, format can give rise to more detail than is productive. Planning should, in one way, be no more than the minutes of the creative application of existing corporate learning to the new scenario. As soon as tedium overtakes value, stop. What a format most usefully does is to jog memory with an agenda for discussion.

Classic headings for a brand plan are:

1. Assumptions, especially any that have changed. Get your excuses in first. These should include relevant changes in consumer values and the economic and social environment, inflation for example. Brevity is vital: bullet points only.
2. Market forecasts. Forecasting competitor strategy if that is both necessary and useful.
3. Brand positioning or target markets and key propositions *
4. Strategy *
5. Product, packaging, quality. +
6. Costs and pricing. +
7. Advertising and PR. +
8. Promotions and merchandizing activity. +
9. Selling and distribution. +

10. Profit summary showing itemized budgets.

* These should, ideally, not change from year to year. When they do, the change needs highlighting with clear analysis and justification.

+ The components of the marketing mix can be structured in many different ways. This is only one list. Each should consider: I Lessons from prior year(s). II Competitor activity both current and forecast. III Any shift in policy, with analysis and justification if so. IV Specific actions. Who will do what and when. V Cost/benefits of those actions, i.e. measurable outcomes. How do we know if we are doing well or badly? We may need to be clear about any outcomes that exceed or fall short of the original objectives set.

In a single market every brand plan may justify increased expenditure on grounds of increased market share.

This format is shorter than some recommend. A final plan may be 20–30 pages. The items omitted are:

1. *Executive summary.* Generally a good business practice but not strictly necessary here. The profit plan IS the executive summary. For that reason it might begin the plan.
2. *Economic and social environment.* This is the same for all brands and gives rise to some of the key assumptions. A separate document is one way to prevent too much carbohydrate in each brand plan. Few environmental changes directly impact marketing actions. Include them in 'assumptions' only if they do.
3. *Current marketing situation.* Endless pages of what readers already know. Delete.
4. *Strengths and weaknesses (SWOT) analysis.* Some practitioners love them; others include such analysis only where appropriate. See chapter on competition.
5. *Objectives.* Contentious this but redundant. Objectives, goals or targets should be set before the plan is written. They will usually come from the longer-term corporate planning process, good or bad, and help direct the marketing planning

process. Some, nevertheless, find it helpful to recapitulate the objectives within the plan.

Senior management needs to develop wisdom in reviewing plans that claim more than ever results. Does that make the decisions to proceed wrong? No. Unless one expects to win, one will not even come second. Much marketing is running very hard to stand still in relative terms. A standing still plan would not, rightly, be accepted so we go through the ritual of planning high but accepting less.

## 4. HARNESSING FINANCE AND SYSTEMS SUPPORT

Serious planners may find this unprofessional, but a short cut is to keep the word-processing disk of last year's plan. Just alter it up to this year's. Show the changes.

The reconciliation of the numbers within the plan, i.e. internal consistency, is also simple if the plan is short and incremental. What is not simple, in a large organization, is the reconciliation of the differing forecasts and plans from the other business functions. Furthermore, the outcome of the planning process needs to be spread across accounting periods and budget centres so that the plan numbers can be compared with the actual results as they come through.

If the marketing manager is left with this role, as many are, demotivation will follow. The planning process will lose value as the business of producing a physical document takes over from analysis and innovation.

The relationship between marketing and finance may be seen as poachers and gamekeepers. Better is for finance to be fully involved. Interest the financial staff in the provision of information that supports and improves marketing plans rather than simply controlling expenditure.

Companies should demystify. Teach marketing to accountants and accounting to marketers. Bring information systems specialists and accountants into the marketing processes. The marketer will be delighted provided the numerical chores of number crunching and data entry can be taken over by those functions.

Companies that have made this transition have noted the change of attitudes that results. Finance classically regards marketing as a black hole of unregulated expenditure. The plan is attacked when it is all but final. Marketers react defensively. The control aspects of the plan, i.e. variances between plan and actual, may be presented critically. Confusion results from differences between various plan numbers.

Full participation, using improved information systems, by finance will not bring choirs of angels but it will reduce negatives in the planning process.

## 5.  THE PLANNING CYCLE

Planning processes acquire redundant routines the way a ship attracts barnacles. Perhaps a one-off question has been made permanent or research is routinely re-visited. Is the timing of the planning cycle still right? Streamlining the planning process needs to take place before bringing new technology to bear. A plan is simply the synthesis of management's intentions. Those intentions need to be brought together as close to the moment for action as possible. A plan that is ready months before the action is needed, should be re-visited. A plan that is too early or too late is a waste of effort.

The ideal planning cycle should be dictated by the seasonality of the business. Working backwards, the timing of actions should dictate the date of the plan, the prior analysis and back to measurement. The planning cycle should be determined by the market and not by the financial year of the corporation. That is rarely recognized.

Planning should not be a dry as dust rendition of words and numbers on paper. It should a lively interchange between all those involved in building the brand and the profits of the company. The plan should record the conclusions reached in order to provide performance indicators but more importantly as the base plate for corporate learning. We learn by trying and discovering what works. The planning process records what will happen and carries the learning forward from year to year and one group of managers to another. If the process outlined here is followed in principle, then plans will automatically be integrated. The format is used as an agenda for creative discussions between the managers in the company with the knowledge, expertise and relevant commitment. The plan itself is simply the minutes of that agreement.

- **MEMO TO FILE**

*Subject:* PRAGMATIC PLANNING

- Planning is integral to corporate learning. Yes, it is a means to control but that is the lesser part. Use the planning process to encourage creativity, innovation, participation and commitment. A plan is a book of numbers, not a romantic novel. Yet the process, if it is well done, should produce that passion necessary to achieve more than anyone first considered possible.

- A fixed skeleton format may look as if planning is reduced to filling in boxes. Use one just the same to jog the memory. You may not need all the textbook headings of the marketing mix. You will need lessons from prior year, analysis, strategy, actions and budget.

- Use the company information systems to help keep numbers consistent both internally in the plan and with all other planning and control systems in the company. Product managers should not be used as number crunchers or keyboard operators. Encourage full participation by Finance.

- Revisit the planning timetable. Is it determined by the market? How close to the action can you plan?

# 26. Quality is in the eye of the beholder

**ISSUES:**

1. Relative perceived quality is best indicator of profitability.
2. The salami principle.
3. Quality management needs precise measurement. The Japanese experience.

## 1. DOES QUALITY MATTER TO MARKETERS?

It was Emerson who suggested that if you built a better mousetrap, the world would beat a path to your door. Marketers scoff: how would customers know it was there? Publicity creates markets, they claim. Awareness drives demand through packaging, advertising and promotion. Low cost production, mass marketing and economies of scale fuel the competitive pricing that creates high market share; profits will follow.

There developed a conventional wisdom that the market leader would also be the most profitable. The second brand would be profitable enough but there were few, if any, prizes for the unplaced horses. Examples can always be found to justify this type of judgement. Academic research is ambiguous; market share may or may not be a predictor of relative profitability. It is true that brand leaders are more likely to be profitable than the laggards but the relationship is weak. More probably they are both correlated with perceived product quality, perceived, that is to say, by the consumer.

There is a circularity in this: consumers express their preferences in what they buy. The sheer numbers of purchases would therefore indicate a vote for the brand leader as being seen to be better. You do not need expensive market research, still less marketing professors, to tell you that.

Two developments blew the whistle on the numbers game: the conversion of Japanese production from low cost imitation to high quality innovation, and the recognition that price was a stronger indicator of quality than market share. Before looking at these, it is worth reviewing why marketing has created the modern concept of quality so that quality, in turn, could create the modern concept of marketing.

Now let's go round that loop a little more gently.

In Victorian times, quality was known to be important; new wealth had created a demand for better rather than more. Quality could be measured in terms of weight, thickness, strength and/or delicacy. In this pre-Einstein age, quality was self-evident and absolute. Sometimes 'more' meant less as in more refined or finer fabrics, but it was still measurable in terms of the product itself.

Quality could therefore be defined numerically. Men in white coats could inspect production to guarantee satisfactory standards were set. Tolerance of the sub-standard was not a Victorian virtue.

Enter the marketers. From their point of view the product could be anything the consumers, and in the meanwhile the customers, wanted. If they preferred lighter saucepans, give them lighter saucepans whatever the quality inspectors may say. Whatever consumers will pay more for, is better.

Measurement moved from the production line to the marketplace. Since consumers' words are unreliable, researchers devised all kinds of sophisticated methods for establishing perceived quality preferences: blind and double blind trials, inviting consumers to price the alternatives, trading off one feature for another (or 'conjoint analysis', which has a better ring).

This turned out to be a less than precise science. Some of the best examples lie in the beer industry. In the UK, Watneys caught the marketing virus in the late 60s. Draught bitter had recently progressed from what reactionaries now call real beer to pasteurized liquid with the fizz injected from cylinders supplied by British Oxygen. It was symbolized by the transition from wooden barrels to metal kegs. By objective measures the beer reached the consumer in better condition and wastage was dramatically reduced. Flowers had led the way. Watneys hastened to catch up with 'Red Barrel'. With hindsight, it was unwise to draw attention to what proved to be a negative feature but brewers believed at the time that consumers preferred it. Research had indicated that consumers could not distinguish between the two brews. The better keeping quality was thus a bonus.

The previous management generation might have listened to their instincts and to the publicans, but the modern marketers knew better. As relations and communications with the publicans deteriorated for other reasons, Watneys conducted more and more professional research. They could improve on 'Red Barrel' with a sweeter, cheaper, lower proof beer to be called 'Watneys Red'. Research showed that consumers prefered it. The image makers were turned loose. Footprints appeared all over town leading to signs saying 'Red is Coming'. The Hippodrome (now Talk of the Town) nightclub staged the launch to the sales force. Some had a premonition of what was coming but not the chairman who had donned a most elegant pair of red socks for the occasion.

Watneys Red was a disaster. The more discerning, i.e. more loquacious, bitter drinker in the pub was already mocking Red Barrel. Watneys Red proved his point. In a focus group, maybe, he could not tell the difference, but with his buddies in the pub he certainly could. The word of mouth is more powerful than the best advertising; and as it turned out, the advertising compounded the problem with a slickness and jokiness that further detracted from the seriousness of the beer. That traditional English bitter is serious whilst lager is a matter for levity may be a generalization too far, but it seemed to be true then.

As it happened, the disaster coincided with Watneys' acquisition by GrandMet. New management moved in to cut the brand, repair publican relationships, reduce advertising and restore the quality. Twenty years on, and with the help of widespread distribution through their own pubs, Watneys beers have finally regained a grudging acceptance.

A similar story happened in the USA. Budweiser and Schlitz had struggled neck and neck since prohibition days. In the mid 70s Budweiser was ahead but not by much. (The business had been taken over by the Busch family 100 years previously; the fourth generation August Busch, was now at the helm.) Both brewers had between 15 and 20 per cent of the market. Today Budweiser and its associated beers have half the total domestic beer market. Schlitz has virtually disappeared. Unlike Watneys, Schlitz had no retail estate to give it a second chance when it lost its name for quality, the opposition was tougher and the mistakes may have been worse. But the parallel with Watneys was strong. Schlitz found ways to reduce the maturing time for beer and to change the formulation. Both saved money and the consumers, in research, could not tell the difference. In reality, they started talking. August Busch, by contrast, is seen to make a fetish of his conservative, demanding adherence to old values and standards. Whether he really does or not is beside the point. That is what the consumer believes and, more importantly, wants to believe. By the time the Schlitz company returned the beer to its original quality and standards, it was too late. The consumer's mind, once made up about quality, is hard to shift. Examples are not limited to beer. All over the world, marketers were conducting usage and attitude studies on their brands and being satisfied by the quality results and by the changes they were making.

## 2.  THE SALAMI PRINCIPLE

Both beer examples illustrate 'the salami principle'. This well known American metaphor refers to the practice of taking such thin slices off the sausage that the sausage each time appears unchanged. One day there is no sausage left. Marketing moved the focus for determining quality from the production line to the marketplace. That was good. Unfortunately marketing's techniques were not up to the job of measuring quality once it arrived. The salami slices are often too thin.

The last ten years have seen a rediscovery of quality and what it means. The recognition that the better mousetrap does indeed provide the path to riches is changing the shape of marketing. The brand manager is no longer mesmerized by a better advertising campaign, but by a substantial product improvement from R&D. Marketers are taking more interest in the value the consumer receives. To return to the loop, marketing has changed the perception of quality which in turn has changed the perception of marketing. Marketing seeks to add value for the consumer and, in so doing, add profitability for the brand owner. To do that the salami principle has to be reversed.

## 3. THE JAPANESE EXPERIENCE

Many have commented on the irony that the prophet who gave the quality mission to the Japanese only did so because he was without honour in his own land, the USA. Rarely can compatriots have been so burnt. The key to the mission was this consistent thread: *quality can be measured.* How to measure it may call for imagination, trial and error but, without measurement, continuous consistent improvement is impossible. It takes westerners many more syllables to express what the Japanese call *Kai Zen.* Deming found a country already prepared for his approach to quality both culturally, physically and economically; physically because the space in their homes does not allow for more, only better, and economically because of the recognition that increasing incomes would also lead to demands for premium goods. When Deming arrived shortly after World War II, all that was in the future.

There is one Japanese characteristic, however, that was crucial to success and has been less documented. They will think this impolite but the word 'arrogance' is used in admiration. Arrogance is admirable because it works. Research on consumers' preferences are affected in three ways:

1. Japanese marketers assume, without asking, that a Japanese consumer will want the best. Only the best deserve the best.
2. Because of the much greater sharing of culture and values the marketer has a better idea of the consumer's point of view before asking. The market is more homogenous, at least in the cities.
3. If Japanese consumers think it is the best, so will everyone else in the world once it is explained to them.

Such self confidence pays. It means that the Japanese producer is better able to anticipate what the consumer will find valuable and believes, rightly or wrongly, that once the domestic market buys it, so will the rest of the world. The Victorian English behaved similarly in consumer technological products. They have been proved more right than wrong.

What came out of the great quality success stories is a blind faith, which then proves to be right. Can this be marketing? People driven by Messianic fervour tend not to stop for a little conjoint analysis. Can such apparent disregard for consideration of the consumer be commercial? Speculative it is and yet quality-oriented marketers may be achieving a critical identification with consumer values. Forget market research carried out by a bunch of cranks on consumers who do not know what they are talking about.

A famous and successful magazine publisher was once asked how he managed to launch title after title with so few failures. His research team must be excellent. It turned out that he had no team and no research. He was a compulsive watcher of television; and that told him all he needed to know about consumer interests.

'Would I like it better?' is a perfectly reasonable question to ask. Then make it and market it at a higher price than the competition. If it sells and resells, the chances are that it is indeed seen as better. As we have discussed elsewhere, price and perceptions of quality are bound up with one another. A consumer will give a higher priced article the benefit of the doubt on quality until proven otherwise. Such proof can come in any number of ways: beer drinkers in the pub, newspaper or magazine reviews, poor usage experience, appearance in discount stores or coupons, inappropriate marketing are some of them. But beware, the combination of high price and damaged reputation can be lethal.

On the other hand, high price supported by perceived quality spells high profits. They reinforce one another. Quality does not necessarily cost more; getting rid of inspectors, rejects, wastage and attributes not valued by consumers may even reduce costs. All you have to do is to see things through the eyes of the consumer.

- **MEMO TO FILE**

*Subject:* QUALITY

- What do I have to do to tune into consumers' perceptions of my brands and competitors'? Focus groups? Trade fairs? Market visits?

- This is only the beginning. You have to anticipate what consumers will want, something they themselves do not know. There is, therefore, no point in asking. Project your anticipation; then see if it sells.

- The salami principle will reduce quality unless you reverse it. Do not pare value surreptitiously down but find small ways to show the consumer that value is being added.

$$\boxed{Q}$$

# 27. Quantity

**ISSUE:**

1.  Do you really want more volume?

More is better. This is not greed; one is not seeking more oneself. We managers are but puppets of the stock markets; quarterly figures are a treadmill manipulated by some greater being. Really? Who believes that? Crying into a Martini is unlikely to convince anyone that marketers are not out for all they can get. More volume translates into more cash into more profits.

It is worth pausing a moment to question this assertion. After all, why trouble to sell 10 widgets for $1 each when you can sell one for $10? The perfume industry limits distribution, and thus sales volume, in order to prop up the price. Even more impressively, it has persuaded Brussels to bless the arrangements, although the UK is reviewing them.

Economists assume there is a trade-off between price and volume along the classic curve we saw earlier under Pricing.

We have considered elsewhere the effect price has on the perception of quality: it is possible to increase both price AND volume but not often. But what the classic price/quantity trade-off implied by the curve really fails to account for is the longer

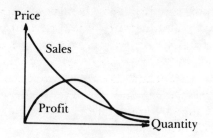

*Figure 19   Prices and volumes*

term effect: a higher price today, if it is positive in terms of brand image, will be beneficial for sales tomorrow.

Similarly, whilst higher sales today can be beneficial for future volumes, there are many cases where the reverse is true. For example:

1. *Supply or demand is limited.* A widget sold is a widget less to sell. For durables one would maintain high prices on innovation, were it not for competition, and only reduce them slowly as demand at each price level was satisfied. On the basis that a family buys only once, the aim has to be to maximize the profit on that single sale.

2. *'Scarcity marketing' is the delicate business of creating shortages in order to stimulate demand.* Some take credit for this technique to cover up forecasting errors. The launch of Wilkinson Sword stainless steel razor blades in the 1960s was an example of this technique; whether deliberate or accidental, the publicity surrounding the initial shortages fuelled both reputation and future sales.

   Scarcity marketing has to be credible. The launch of Tanqueray Sterling Vodka in the USA in 1989 included publicity for the thousands of cases that had to be air-freighted from the UK to meet unprecedented demand. Sceptics predominated over the convinced, and the brand failed.

3. *Money-off promotions.* As discussed in a previous chapter, controversy surrounds the net benefits of these techniques.

If consumers simply phase their purchases to meet the promotions, total volumes are unaffected. Brand loyalists are likely to be in this category, while brand switchers will move to the promoted brand. If all brands promote equally, the net volume effect may still be neutral and profits reduced all around. The main area of controversy surrounds the impact of promotions on brand image: by devaluing the brand, longer term sales may decrease.

- **MEMO TO FILE**

*Subject:* QUANTITY

- Chasing volume can weaken brand equity, i.e. long-term profitability, and even short-term. It can diffuse efforts and perceptions. Do we really want more volume? If so, how much?

# R

# 28. Search and Research

**ISSUES:**

1. Understanding the market is so totally crucial that any new CEO should get out the broom for a thorough sweep.
2. Clear away special interests.
3. Establish what is available. A summary of market research methods.
4. Challenge what you do now.

## 1. UNDERSTANDING THE MARKET

Market research reminds one of badges on a boy scout. The more you have the more proficient you must be. Searching out the key information on customers and consumers needed by decision-makers soon leads to a fascinating jungle. Have you ever intended to make one search in a library and then found the side tracks more interesting?

Research reveals that 24 per cent of all women (in the UK, 1987 figures) have no teeth. Not your experience? Does it matter?

The great marketing companies have so much research that some explorers have not been seen for years. Before a multimillion dollar decision, the marginal cost of just a little more data is minimal. The analysis → paralysis problem is not new and has been widely addressed. It is a good place to start because the biggest companies have too much research, or the wrong sort. Others have too little. No one has just the right amount. If in doubt, research the issue to find out!

The result is greatly increasing research budgets but not necessarily better decisions. It is time to compare what you really want to know with what you have and whether you believe it.

Grappling with research is complicated by the mixed motivations of the others involved, notably market research professionals and advertising agencies. They would really like research to solve your problems. They just believe it would be nice if it met their own interests along the way. It is a tough position to maintain but there is no substitute for ensuring that market research is truly independent and arms length. Do not, for example, allow your advertising agency to commission the research on its own work.

Market research is supposed to supply the diagnostics you need for your marketing efforts. You cannot rely on third parties. What do you do? Take the plunge and make three moves:

- Move A: Clear away special interests.
- Move B: Establish what is available.
- Move C: Challenge what you do now.


## 2. MOVE A: CLEAR AWAY SPECIAL INTERESTS

If you have internal market research professionals, sack them. Be nice by all means. Set them up in their own or one of your new agencies but sack them. Outsourcing market research is unlikely to be more expensive. It will give a much better chance of finding what you need to know. This is not a polemic against researchers. Far from it. When lost in the jungle, one is grateful to the boy scout who can find south by bisecting the hour hand

and the sun and rub necessities together. Research is a highly professional activity. It is not for amateurs.

As your pen hovers over the dismissal notices, voices will tell you that you need your internal specialists to identify the top outsiders and keep them up to the mark. Assessing professionals needs professional skills. You need some on your side. Others will say that an in-depth understanding of the business is vital. Only your inside market research experts can marry your practical business considerations together with the technical. Sign the papers.

## 3. MOVE B: ESTABLISH WHAT IS AVAILABLE

You need your own rough guide to the terrain. You are learning enough to ask the questions even if you do not understand the answers.

Establishing some general patterns of research does not involve technicalities. Appendix I has some jargon for the bold to surprise the experts. There is a risk, like trying out your Dutch in Holland, that their responses may bewilder, but test them anyway.

Businesses are not as different as they think they are. Though too polite to say so, researchers should have seen the problems before. If they haven't, you may have the wrong professionals. If they cannot quickly relate to the issues you are trying to resolve, and explain everything in language you can understand, you have the wrong professionals. If on the other hand they are too quick to open up the tool-kit before they have really understood the problem they are certainly the wrong lot. Some travel with only one or two tools they hope will fit everything. Researchers are only plumbers after all.

There are two types of general pattern to establish:

● What kinds of research are there?
● What decisions are assisted by what research?

*What types of market research are there?*

The convention has emerged that one can divide research into two types: qualitative and quantitative. The former indicates what might matter; the other is supposed to measure the extent to which it does. Qualitative spends time with only a few respondents but in great depth. Rather over ten per cent of research expenditure is spent this way. The balance is spent on quantitative research, opinion polls for example. It goes into very little depth but questions a large number of people.

Far the most popular qualitative type is the group discussion, or focus group. Usually six, seven or eight members of roughly the same demographic group (i.e. age, sex, class, I mean socio-economic group) are recruited for an hour or two of gentle conversation. The money is good and it helps if the surroundings are too. The need to relax is paramount. Do not mix your groups and get rid of disruptive elements at once. Professional facilities include taping (video and/or audio) the proceedings and a one-way mirror to conceal non-participants. These facilities are always explained to the respondents. I have never known them to object. Quite quickly they are forgotten.

Discussion is led, usually, by a trained psychologist from the general to the specific. At this point opinions diverge on how focus groups should be used. Some find them unreliable.

One theory is to run many different groups until some consensus emerges and then do some quantitative research. The scientific method identifies all the variables, pins some down and ruthlessly analyses the rest. Only that way can you be sure. Such certainty may be expensive because it is as certain as the horse you were given in the pub last night. It may work but wiser counsel is to save your money.

Drunks use lamp-posts for support, not illumination. Decision-makers that need this much support should not be out on the street. Discussion groups are wonderful for providing illumination. Consumers talking about your brands and marketing ideas will put into a single sentence, occasionally, all the insight you need to have. Just one statement by one consumer might be the revelation that unlocks millions. So be there. The psychologist will miss the nuances. He or she does not know your business. Several weeks later a 20 page report, which the one-way onlooker would have a job to recognize, will drop through your letter box. Do not blame the psychologist. It is the nature of the role. Some marketers are so enthusiastic about discussion groups, they train to become group leaders. Away from the world's research centres, in third world situations, that may be the only solution but the roles are better separate.

We have lingered on discussion groups as the primary building block of market research. They are used for new brands and changes to existing ones: positioning, products, packaging, advertising concepts, promotional ideas. Beware that word 'concept' though. Few consumers can give reliable responses to anything except tangible reality they have experienced or can see in front of them. Future possibilities are opaque. Show a real advertisement, not a sketch, even if production costs serious money.

If one cannot limit oneself to a single tangible product or package or advertisement, then use two. Compare only like with like. Expect only the simplest of responses. Sophisticated exercises, such as rank ordering, risk decreasing reliability.

These are some bespoke services. The list is indicative, not comprehensive:

- **Placement tests** leave products, or whatever, for consumers to try in their regular consumption pattern.
- **Personal interviews** track brand usage, awareness, attitudes, what product attributes contribute what to quality, both for you and the competition. They may be pre-arranged or 'intercepts' in shopping areas. Traditionally the interviewer or the respondents themselves will complete a formatted questionnaire. A newer technique is to capture answers electronically.
- **Observation studies**, as the name implies, elicit consumer behaviour without questioning. Eliminates rationalizing, up to a point, by the consumer but has obvious limitations.
- **Telephone interviews** allow questioning in less depth but at greater speed and less expense.

There are various high tech options, mostly controversial. Eye cameras were discussed under Advertising. Electronically wired 'shops' provide observation of choices, notably for testing prices.

All the above are tailormade to your needs and aim to reproduce the marketplace as closely as possible.

Many other facilities are available on a wholly or partly syndicated basis. Questions can be added to general 'omnibus' surveys, e.g. Gallup.

Shared or syndicated services in the UK include:

- **Target Group Index (TGI):** huge annual survey of consumer usage patterns by media, product category and brand.
- **Retail distribution, sales and consumer databases**. Neilsen is the best known of a number of suppliers in this area. Originally a way to track retail level sales by adjusting purchases with changes in inventory. Electronic point-of-sale tills now make far richer data available. Better still consumer panellists simply have to swipe their magnetic card through the reader to log all their purchases. No more checking consumer cupboards and garbage bins as used to be the case. Marketers may now, if they wish, monitor the results of advertising or promotion directly on their targets' shopping baskets. The difference between direct marketing and broadcast is shrinking.

  The traditional use for Neilsen was not for marketing, the numbers were too aggregated and late to be much help. The regional analysis allowed the marketing managers to beat up the sales force, one of their few opportunities for sadism. Just because the numbers can now be both precise and timely, do not expect such a popular blood sport to disappear.

- **Media expenditure:** MEAL (press and TV.); OSCAR (roadside posters); RBL (bus posters); TRAC (London Underground).
- **Media readership/circulation:** ABC, JICNARS (press); BARB (TV); JICRARS (radio).

In short, the UK has more marketing data around than anyone is likely to need.

## What decisions need marketplace information, either regularly or every now and then?

There is some merit in worrying first about the big expenditures. Large advertising expenditures should be benchmarked for awareness and attitude shifts. A big marketing expenditure should not result in pro rata or heavy research budgets. It has to be decision driven: what are my options, what is the most ingenious (i.e. cost/beneficial) way of assessing the options, how credible will the research be when it arrives? This is not to suggest that one should be cheap or skimp research. What is done needs to be high in quality. With increasing quantities of data around, the difficulty is to select what really matters.

Textbooks begin the marketing planning process with a blank page. Businesses begin with last year's plan or whatever is happening now. The team which agreed to the present activities is, short of a crisis, only going to agree incremental changes next time around. A crisis is a crisis because the awful facts are staring you in the face. If the ship is at 45° and going down, skip the testing of assumptions. If your ship is proceeding well enough, then list the incremental changes you could make, i.e. those the team might agree. There are unlikely to be many. Incrementalism has the huge advantage that both decisions and the relevant information can be kept to human proportions.

What do you need to know to decide each one? Can it be researched? Cost? Would you believe it? Is it worth it? One can go potty worrying about all these questions. We mostly have to get on with priorities as they emerge. It just helps to worry a little more than we do.

Clearly research which provides the wrong answers is bad. One is better off without it. The more difficult question is when is inadequate information worse than none? Statisticians have batteries of formulae for assessing adequacy.

Unsophisticated statisticians' figures do not allow for the business experience held by the combined marketing team. The figures are beautiful logic but independent of the problem. That is their strength and their weakness. All that intuition your team has built up should have given a head start even a modicum of new work may be enough.

'Bayesian' statisticians (see Appendix 1, Research Terminology) will build management's prior knowledge into their formulae but that sophistication can complicate the analysis beyond the benefit.

Never mind the numbers, research for illumination. Then call a halt. Luckily you have no internal research professionals to dispute the point.

## 4. MOVE C: CHALLENGE WHAT YOU DO NOW

Much research comes rolling in because no one said stop. Sometimes no decision is expected to need the research but comparative figures might be needed one day. Granny's attic has nothing on research files. Challenging research needs will tell you a great deal about your business and how marketing works in your business.

Most of all challenge the use of research as support for decisions. Decisions are about the **future**; research can only tell you about **now**. It is especially dangerous in the fashion area. Research will tell you, for example, that consumers only like pink whatevers and hate blue ones most of all. By the time your pink product hits the streets, only blue will do. Furthermore all your competitors are researching the same market in the same way and coming to the same conclusions. When you get to the marketplace you will have to share what is left of the pink business with them.

## 5. WHERE HAVE THESE THREE MOVES LEFT US?

Whether you save money, gain insights or commission additional research, these three moves should increase wisdom and profits. Or one of them anyway. There are no rules of thumb for research expenditure but you might start worrying if you are still spending more than 5 per cent or less than 2 per cent of your marketing budget, if it is a big one, on market research. But do not worry long. It is too serious a subject to take seriously. If you do no research at all, you will either hit the right answer (by chance) or do something different (good).

- **MEMO TO FILE**

*Subject:* SEARCH AND RESEARCH

- Seek illumination, not support. At best, research can only reveal the present, not the future.

- Use only external top professionals.

- Understanding consumers is the key. Discussion groups are the door. Be there when it opens.

- Challenge research expenditure. You may wind up spending more but it will be worth it.

- Your competitors are accessing the same information. Might you be reaching the same conclusions?

$$\boxed{\text{S}}$$

# 29.   Segmentation

**ISSUES:**

1. Tools for increased profits and/or better use of marketing resources.
2. Demassifying marketing through more precise information. Getting riches from niches.
3. Complexity versus benefit.

## 1.   FOCUSING RESOURCES FOR BETTER EFFORT

Segmentation divides a market into groups of consumers with similar needs or in some other way that allows the marketer to focus separately. Concentrating on a limited market marshals resources. Segmentation takes many forms: language, ethnic groups, sex, locality and age group are but five ways of grouping consumers. More sophisticated segmentation involves psychographic measures of life styles, loyalty factors and whether consumers are trendsetters, followers or whatever. Price, size of packaging, flavours and product characteristics are brand attributes that can be used to partition markets. Occasions of use may define still other segments. In all cases the marketer is recognizing that consumers are different. Even if she could market directly to all the world in one go, it would not be economic to do so.

An airline fills a plane through price discrimination. Those prepared to fly First Class do so. Those who need to book ahead pay more than those ready to chance standby. A single plane may carry customers who have paid a dozen or more different prices for their seats. The airline maximizes its profit by persuading each group of people to pay the most before opening its doors to the next cheapest group. So long as no one pays less than the marginal cost of the seat (minimal) the airline wants to fill every seat.

To achieve this, an airline erects 'walls of discrimination' in order that the price differences are legitimate. A ticket that requires the customer to return after the weekend, for example, will be attractive to holiday-makers but not to business travellers. The sophistication of computer systems in allocating seats to the different fare categories and helping airline sales people juggle the remaining vacancies can distinguish the profitable airline from the loss-maker.

Segmentation theory divides consumers into like clusters so that marketing can be neatly and relevantly focused. Virginia Slims were the first cigarette to be successfully targeted to women. The classic segmentation for the international marketer is by geography, i.e. national boundaries. Global marketing takes segmentation across boundaries. The entertainment industry, for example, will target by age group for music or films worldwide.

Segmentation is essential for a new brand to gain a beachhead. Defining a narrow section of the population simplifies positioning, distribution and the marketing mix. As the brand grows in popularity within the chosen segment, the marketer is faced by a choice of continuing to increase share in the original segment or widening the target. Premature expansion can be as deathly as lingering in the first segment whilst others take over the expansion.

One of the most successful US airlines, Delta, owes its profitability to its historical dominance of the Atlanta traffic. In 1988 it had about 11 per cent of the US airline market defined by passenger miles. Yet with about half the Atlanta traffic it was able to exert considerable leverage on consumers within that segment as well as achieving economies through localized services.

This illustrates the dangers of using market share as a forecaster of profitability. Which market applies? Nevertheless, a larger share of a smaller market is likely to be more profitable than a smaller share of a larger market. This strategy plus the benefits of price discrimination cause today's marketers to look more closely at customization.

Manufacturers are abandoning mass production in order to add value by tailoring products, if not to individual customers, then to market niches. The earliest example of this as a counter-trend was the development of General Motors. Ford through the universality of the Model T dominated the post World War I market. General Motors was put together from a hotchpotch of independent companies but rapidly became a family of brands each positioned for one segment of the market. By outflanking Ford, Alfred Sloan took over market leadership.

More recently, Ernest Saunders faced the same problem when Guinness acquired the DCL. Their whisky brands were undifferentiated and competed largely with each other. The marketing task was to give them separate targets, positioning and segments.

Recently, researchers have argued that there is no such thing as a niche brand; there are only big brands and small brands. Pursuit of the niche brand, they say, is a dangerous mirage: a small brand has fewer customers who buy the brand less often. This is called Double Jeopardy.

Those who believe in niche brands may be shocked by the finding but the issue is largely semantic. The term 'niche brand' comes from the concept of hiding away from more powerful competitors. Through careful segmentation and differentiation a brand such as Aqua Libra is in a 'niche', or shelter, compared to Schweppes Tonic.

The avoidance of competition is an important marketing concept. Charles Darwin (how's that for pedigree!) used the word niche in the evolution of species in the same way marketers do. As brands are just another species, in Darwinian terms, the usage is appropriate.

What the Double Jeopardy research indicates is not the absence of niche brands but the lack of loyalty to specialist brands that their owners expected. In looking at such matters markets have to be carefully defined.

## 2. USING MORE PRECISE INFORMATION

By linking computer systems from point-of-sale through to production lines, it is now possible to produce to differing specifications on the same line so that specialist demands can be met with minimal production inefficiencies or inventory carrying costs.

Segmentation may also arise to met the needs of retailers and the distribution system. Duty free shopping at airports is more attractive to the consumer if it appears to be a 'deal'. The consumer's expectation is, of course, to save duty. The reality is that the duty saving is much less, on premium goods, than the increase in margins that the shop has to pay the airport authority. To some extent the duty free shopper can be separately segmented both in terms of the shopper and the product being offered. Many perfumes and high priced spirits are either not available on the High Street or only at artificial prices, i.e. for show, not for sale. Offering marginally different products to provide walls of discrimination so that retailers can price differently has a long history.

Information systems have brought new dynamics to niche marketing, distribution and production. Direct marketing uses databases to select appropriate customers for quite low volume brands. Some services work the other way about: the consumer can search product and supplier databases both for the brands she wants and also the best terms.

The potential information available on each consumer is enormous and will grow with use. At the beginning the marketer can specify the target and the computer can prepare mail to go to those consumers that match the specification, or a list of numbers to be telephoned. Even the call can be automated so that the consumer interacts with the computer direct. As the pattern of consumer orders builds up, it becomes easier to forecast the type of purchase the consumer may make. Those who order often, spend a great deal, and have done so recently are prioritized by the computer system.

Some consider this new world with horror. The database marketers, however, claim that consumers far prefer the tailoring of offers to their likely needs to the junk mailings of the past. Where the process is consumer initiated there can be little doubt that it can offer substantial advantages over trailing around shops filled with the product in the wrong colour or the wrong trim. It is no more than a technological development of mail order services which have been available for a century. In the United States special kiosks are made available for those without home computer or suitable hardware.

Marketing matches consumers with brands. What was done in the mass can now be done, with electronic help, more precisely. The trick is to get riches from niches.

## 3.  COMPLEXITY

Segmentation is a key part of the trend to demassifying marketing. It allows brands to differentiate themselves within both the market as a whole and the manufacturers' portfolio. In toothpaste, one brand may appeal to the health conscious, another to those seeking the whitest teeth, another to a desire for healthy gums and another to those who want a deal on price. Through the use of factor analysis and cluster analysis, each market can be separately identified and quantified. The effects of specific marketing programmes on specific clusters can, up to a point, be measured. Perhaps more importantly, the marketer can identify with the particular segment she is addressing. The more precisely one can 'see' the consumer in the mind's eye, the better the presentation of benefits can be.

Not everything is positive. The identification of a particular brand, and especially a new brand, with its segment is vital. To target a mature brand, however, to different segments in different ways may be complex. The marketing team, the sales force, the agencies all have to remember which is which and distinguish the activities. Some companies divide the roles: one agency might deal with the 'value' segment and message whilst another looks after the 'health' message, for example. Dividing the activities loses economies of scale and can confuse consumers. It is not possible to use mass media in a niche way.

Nevertheless, segmentation is a powerful weapon in the battle to get more from less marketing spending. Choosing between segments in terms of their response rates to marketing programmes can achieve higher profits by concentrating growth in areas of strength and then using that increased strength progressively as a springboard for wider segments.

- **MEMO TO FILE**

*Subject:* SEGMENTATION

- Segmentation is the key to improved value for money from the marketing budget. Focus on the target defined by consumer group, product attributes and occasions of use can maximize strength in that segment.

- Having achieved critical mass within the chosen segment, it can be broadened or extended.

- The disadvantage of segmentation is the complexity of differing programmes for the same brand. The theoretical benefits have to be balanced against the planning, execution and control on-costs.

# 30. Training marketing professionals: sorry, but we've done that

**ISSUE:**

1. Marketing training can improve performance both of trainers and trainees, but change the focus from training to learning. Cross fertilize best practice.

The most important assets of many companies are their brands. Many others without major brands still depend on marketing for their existence and prosperity. Increasing the value of those brands, outwitting the competition, dominating the market-place, all these critical functions are led by the company's marketing professionals. These people spend huge sums on advertising, merchandizing and promotion. The result can be huge profits, but there are no precise ways of linking the two. Companies have to depend on the finely honed instincts and experience of their marketing people. They tend to come from the younger cadre of managers in organizations, so that experience has to be won early or from others. Marketing is a team game with few players. The lean marketing departments of today can afford no weak links. One can visualize the intensity of training necessary for those professionals to stay at the top. One can; but one would be wrong.

R&D people, the accountants, the Human Resource managers, the Junior Assistant Company Secretary have all had more formal training than most marketers. With luck your marketing people will have had some or all of the following:

- A year or so as a sales merchandiser or the equivalent. That is a good start; there is no substitute for the marketplace itself.
- Formal marketing courses teaching the four Ps, usually lasting a week at a time.
- Time in an advertising agency gaining a wonderfully cynical view of the client's strengths and weaknesses. It is also a fine opportunity to study advertising, one of the largest parts of the marketing mix, and its role as a bridge between consumers and brand owners. The immersion in the application of advertising to many product categories is the upside of the Rule of Chi (see chapter 34). The down curve is the life long indulgence to agencies that follows. If you want the best from your agency, it helps not to know too much about them. On the other hand you should train their people to know about your business.
- Books and magazines.
- Experience with a leading marketing company. Serving an apprenticeship with a good marketer has equipped most of today's top marketers with all they needed to know.
- (In the USA) An MBA which followed immediately after the first degree.

Marketing people are bright. They learn fast. Many will say that this form of training is just fine as it is.

Up to about the age 27, that is true. Unfortunately, at that point the training largely stops. Hunter-Miller (a London based executive search agency specializing in senior marketing appointments) researched the leading UK fast moving consumer goods companies in February 1991 and the largest retailers in July. Within the fmcg companies, Hunter-Miller found a high level of dissatisfaction leading to movement amongst marketers in the 28-30 year age group. The marketers themselves were not able to associate cause and effect, but in all cases training had plateaued at about 27. These marketing professionals saw themselves as having had all the training they were likely to get. They felt that the company ceased to be interested in them. Unless promotion was imminent, they looked outside.

That is not to say that they would have accepted additional training had it been offered. By that stage busy, preoccupied and feeling that they have 'arrived', expectations had built up that could not be fulfilled. Disaffiliation resulted.

The loss to the fmcg companies was a gain to the retail grocery sector, which provides little or no marketing training, but relies on the outflow from fmcg. General management training by the retail chains, however, is strong.

Perhaps the lesson from this research has less to do with the motivation of marketers as with the question of why age 27 marks such a barrier to further development. Marketing is the business of managing innovation, and change is constant. Yesterday's sales promotion was fine but it will not work tomorrow.

It is not a matter of offering marketing professionals further development in strategy or finance or general management. That is done in many companies. For those moving into general management, as many do, such training is wholly admirable, but what about marketing itself? And what about more cross-functional training, notably in sales and operations?

Is it any coincidence that information systems which have transformed so many corporate functions have made so little impact on marketing? Ten years may have passed since the most senior professionals in your company last received marketing training. Since then, tills have become electronic, thus opening up masses of data. Can your marketers cope with the new information explosion? How many can tell you about interactive consumer continuity programmes such as the US Catalina Marketing or Vision Value Club? Without continuous training, is it small wonder that marketers fail to keep up to date?

And how many have horizons limited to their own country? 1992 has arrived. The UK domestic market now has 320 million consumers speaking ten languages. North America has a similar

number with the Spanish language and many others gaining
ground. No longer is a single country or culture a valid horizon.
Even a region may be too limited: global is the thing. International marketing needs quite different knowledge, skills, attitudes
and actions to the domestic variety. Are your marketing
professionals ready for that?

Brave new frontiers such as sophisticated information systems
or global marketing make attractive topics for learning. Less
welcome are those old basics we all know but few practice. Back
in the 1960s every brand manager had a brand bible with all the
salient points about his (yes, it was always 'his' in those days)
brand. He lugged it around and referred to it constantly. It
certainly lengthened his arms. His successors now wonder why
he bothered.

The same fate may overtake the brand plan. The textbooks
view it as the cornerstone of marketing yet only a minority of
UK marketing companies have formal brand or marketing
plans. The annual plan is or should be the primary means of
transmitting corporate learning from year to year. It is also the
primary means, in many companies, of training junior marketing management. The process of plan preparation and rejection
is frustrating for all concerned. At the same time corporate
standards, values and, most of all, creativity come from that
process when it is well done.

If the basics are not practised, then the training has not been
effective. Training is not the same as education. (If in doubt on
this point, reflect on whether you would prefer sex education
or sex training.) The word 'training' itself is part of the problem
and should be replaced by something that shifts the focus to
opportunities for learning. Should marketers not be continuously curious about markets, marketing and what others are
doing? Building a climate that encourages learning is not easy
but of great importance.

Some US companies have introduced marketing audits.
Worried by practice being less than professional, visiting
consultants, academics, peers or seniors assess local marketing
processes, standards, whether positioning statements are realistic and so on. The motivation of top management is clear

enough but one wonders what it does for the motivation of the marketers.

Marketing is becoming more visible in boardrooms as volumes falter in recession and the opportunity for cost savings become exhausted. Companies are looking for ways to raise prices and still provide value for money. This is the business of marketing. They are prepared to commit ever greater sums for advertising, merchandizing and promotion but they want them disposed in the most professional fashion. A patchy application of the Four Ps learnt half a generation or more ago will no longer suffice.

At the very least, marketers should be encouraged to learn more from one another. Every company has its share of mavericks who have succeeded and pedants who have added value. Every experienced marketer has something to contribute. Failures are perhaps the best. If marketing is accepted as an art rather than a science, how can those artistic skills be transmitted across boundaries?

● **MEMO TO FILE**

*Subject:* TRAINING MARKETING PROFESSIONALS

● Ask your professionals to take a positive view of learning. What is new? What could it do for them, colleagues, the company?

● Persuade them to share modern marketing theory and practice with their non-marketing colleagues. See how many new books appear on their shelves as a result.

# U

# 31.   The Ugly duckling

**ISSUES:**

1. Truly major breakthroughs can be unrecognized initially.
2. How to create pathways for their development.
3. The need for Champions.
4. Get the ducklings out of research and into the water.

## 1.   RECOGNIZING THE BREAKTHROUGHS

Great brands rarely seem so great at their beginning. In television, Star Trek and Minder performed dismally in their early days. They only just survived. Baileys Irish Cream, today the world's leading liqueur, researched badly and began hesitantly. Early cars were the cause of hilarity. In 1962 the Decca record company rejected the Beatles on the grounds that boys with guitars were outmoded.

It may be going too far to claim that initial failure is a requirement for greatness but successful research should be taken as a warning. Why this is so is explored later in this chapter. Unfortunately disasters also research badly. This is the ugly duckling problem: swans begin as ugly ducklings but so do ugly ducks.

The true parentage of great brands can be obscure. Most companies will only talk about success after the event, ostensibly for commercial security reasons but often because they were just as surprised as the rest of us. In reality this lack of recognition of future winners is a boon to security. It is not necessary to conceal the pearl of the orient if everyone thinks it is a marble. If you want them to think it is a marble, put it in with other marbles. Of course, you may think it is a marble too.

For the great innovation companies, such as 3M, or those, such as Unilever and Procter & Gamble, with horns locked in competition, trying to appear foolish lacks conviction. The rest are quite happy to consider other people's innovation daft. After all, we researched their new brand with negative results. Er, have we forgotten something?

For the moment the veil of discretion can stay over the moment of our ugly duckling's conception and how it got into the wrong pond. There lies the deception. We can all forecast that an ugly duckling swimming around with a Unilever swan is likely to become another Unilever swan. Competitive factors will do their best to knock it out of the water as best they can. The most frequent move is instant imitation. When P&G launched Vizir in Germany after six years' preparation, Henkel, the main competitor, had Liz on the market within days.

Is a noisy launch really to impress the trade or just proud parenthood? Is making a splash the equivalent of passing round cigars (before that became politically incorrect)? Or is it to frighten off the competition?

It is difficult for companies to camouflage their new brands in alien ponds. New brands need constant nurture and attention. There are good reasons for keeping them close by. They need the physical and morale warmth of management and siblings. Some believe in putting new brands out on their own just as Spartans put their babies on the hillsides. The survivors may have been tough but they lost a lot of Spartans.

In the fairy tale, the ugly duckling got into the wrong pond by happenstance. Many great brands owe their existence to a series of mistakes but then, don't we all. It was fortunate, as it turned out, to be swimming with a different crowd. Looking down on this market-place, or pond, what do we see? What distinguishes the ugly duckling?

An ugly duckling:

- Is paddling like hell to get anywhere
- Makes the below the line activity all too visible
- Is awkward and, somehow, doesn't quite fit in. People notice it. Perhaps they laugh at it. Remember how the English mocked the French for drinking bottled water?
- Is unsure about direction or where the next meal is coming from
- Is grateful that the pond is too small for serious threats
- May try to fly but it cannot

Hans Andersen was not a Professor of Marketing (he and Arthur were accountants) but he had the basics right there. Of course every new brand is different and also every product category. This model matches some better than others but compare it with the fully grown great brand:

- It sails serenely along, the object of admiration
- There must be some effort below the line to maintain momentum but it is invisible
- It is graceful and elegant. A swan is always fashionable
- It seems to know where it is going and that you will be casting your bread on the water
- It has no fear of predators. Lesser fowl make way
- It flies majestically

The business of new brands is serious and so is the analogy with procreation. The purpose is the same: companies that do not propagate the species die out.

Glaxo became the leading UK pharmaceutical company on the back of Zantac. Ski yoghourt revitalized Express Dairies. International Distillers and Vintners grew under the GrandMet umbrella from a marginal company in 1974 to the world's largest wine and spirit company largely through acquisitions, but those acquisitions were made possible by the high profits from new brands such as Croft Original, Baileys Irish Cream, Malibu and Piat d'Or. Dunhill became a world brand from a small pipe maker by stumbling into luxury goods for Japan. These are four examples of old companies finding new life from new brands.

Accidental meetings, good luck, people prepared to take risks and groping in the dark play their part in the conception of ugly ducklings just as in other forms of life. New brand development can also be a whole heap of fun.

Every new brand practitioner has built up his own technique from experience. Few agree with one another. They may not even agree with themselves. Successful new brand development owes little to the reapplication of standard formulae as *Police Academy 8* will testify. There must be something of the unexpected in a great new brand, something requiring randomness which any formula will eliminate.

The main reason for new brand development is to maintain the lifeblood of the company. This is not just a matter of profits from the brands themselves. Introducing new brands is invigorating for the company as a whole. It boosts morale and sales force enthusiasm. It wrong foots competition. It is enjoyable. No one in business just for the money deserves it.

## 2.  PATHWAYS FOR NEW BRAND DEVELOPMENT

Whatever the reasons in your company, let us assume that a strategy meeting has taken place. It was agreed that you (being out of the room at the time) would lead the first new brand initiative the company has had in ten years. Giddy with this tribute to your creativity, you reel back to your office and call for coffee. Now what?

Some of the places to begin will be suggested by colleagues, your father-in-law at Sunday lunch (you had forgotten he was coming), your neighbour when you returned the mower (anything to get away from lunch) and your own imagination fevered by the coffee. At one time or another we have tried them all.

The brainstorming concept was invented in the 1950s. Variants have appeared ever since under other names. The idea is to liberate creativity by positive reinforcement. Ideas spark from one member of the group to another. Each one goes one leap of imagination better. Someone writes all the ideas down. The effect can be quite intoxicating, at the time. The only rule is that no criticism or negative comment is allowed. Every idea must be applauded so that the group can progressively think the unthinkable. The process is not unlike awaking from one of those wonderful dreams where you have cracked the secret of the universe, switching on the light and writing it down. In the morning you have to face not only abuse from the other side of the bed but gobbledegook on the telephone message pad. Brainstorming has its place but you should probably move on.

In addition to creating a new brand, your strategy meeting concluded that you were a marketing oriented company or a market oriented company or something like that. Strategy is about direction, not precision. The meeting discussed 'Excellence' and 'Getting closer to customers'. Before getting closer to gins and tonics, the meeting agreed that every member would ride with salesmen for three days a month. If they can spare the time. Contact with top management would be good for the morale of the sales force, a fine team. It is an opportunity to coach the future management of this company. Their ideas will provide fresh thinking straight from the market-place. That is what this company needs. An extemely good note on which to go to lunch. The Chairman had every right to be well pleased.

Your colleagues tell you how lucky you are to have the time to follow up this decision. If only they too could get away from their desks. Three field days later they are proved right. You have had an interesting and refreshing time. It has been very worthwhile. You have learnt a lot. Each of the salesmen agreed that a new brand was essential and knew exactly what was needed. It had an uncanny resemblance to the brand the competition launched last week. Another door closes. And in a recession, when one door closes, another slams in the back draught.

Field visits are exhausting. You are due a spot of hedonism. The Client Service (hah!) Director of your advertising agency is taking you to lunch. Your customers have given you plenty to say and the ad person seems to hang on every word. In truth, she will not hang till they lose the account. You agree that it is wrong to expect salesmen to be creative. Leave that to creative people. Why not turn the new brand problem over to the agency? Why not? Money. This new sense of mutuality, the partnership into the future which arrived with the second bottle of wine, curiously requires only one side to make a down payment.

The likelihood is that your agency is good at advertising but not new brands.

Most think they are and few actually are. There are several reasons. Advertising is ephemeral; new brands are supposed to be eternal. Advertisers are preoccupied with image whereas the thrust needs to be on consumer value. Advertisers are not really in love with their clients or their clients' brands; they are in love with advertising. Brands are just fashion models: not interesting in themselves but for the way they show off the advertising. It is wise indeed to involve the agency in the new brand creation process but rarely is it sensible to turn it over to them.

Lunch was fun and some good thinking came from it. Maybe a professional new brand development agency is the answer. Interviewing the short list is impressive. It is amazing how many brands that seem so long established on supermarket shelves are new to the world in the last fifteen years. Put the best of their professionals on your team.

From here on the process will be influenced by the professionals as well as by a host of category and competitive factors. How long will everything take? How much R&D is involved and what will it cost? What are the costs and leadtime of getting a prototype to market? How can activity be camouflaged from competition?

If the cost of R&D and new prototypes are low, then the competition can be confused by sheer number. Scatter ducklings everywhere and competitors have a problem. Expensive? Yes. Confusing also to sales force and customers? Not if the trial markets are kept small and they understand the game. The critical factor is the cost of prototyping.

Stop. What about looking for a market gap? If you had not

been out with the sales force, not to mention long lunches with advertising and other agencies, the market research manager would have got through to you. In fact, you have been avoiding her calls. Statistics are not for you. You can handle the computer printout and even (standard) deviations but not that unwavering look of certainty.

How long is it since your last U&A (usage and attitude) study? Two years. Eyebrows raise. U&A studies are one of the great earners for market research people.

Market gaps are an attractive idea. Hindsight is on their side. Any new brand fits in somewhere between those that existed before. At the same time there is something odd about the idea that the consumer is waiting for something new to turn up. Ask in any focus group what they want that is not already available and mystification sets in. There are no market gaps out there waiting to be filled. New brands just barge their way into the market, creating gaps for themselves.

By this time your next board meeting is coming up. You have been conspicuously out of the office, put new brand professionals on a retainer and alienated the market research manager by telling her that her wares would not help. The progress report may be brief. Could this be the moment for just in time delegation? A brand manager has joined with impressive skills and a CV that includes new brand development. Innovation requires new blood, new thinking, new ways of looking at things. You are lucky to have someone closer in age and lifestyle to the target market. Wipe the brow. Problem solved.

You are right to put the newcomer on the team. Liaison, progress chasing, tracking the money are going to need more time than you have. Unfortunately, lack of experience of the business/market, i.e. lack of failures, disbars the newcomer. Judgement is more critical than novelty.

Western companies have designed their management hierarchies in such a way that those who have experience cannot apply it. If they are successful they are promoted to ensure they do not do it again. In marketing departments, promotion means being put onto something with a bigger budget, i.e. an established brand. The reality is that managing low budget and new brands is more difficult and yet we give them to managers too junior or too tired to apply the necessary skills.

To summarize the pathway established so far: sales force suggestions and market research have been discounted. The advertising agency, new brand professional and junior marketing manager are on the team but not in charge. Something, or rather someone, is missing.

## 3. THE NEED FOR CHAMPIONS

As we discussed in 'New', the champion concept is usually ascribed to 3M. It is a manager, probably senior but not from that part of the business, who has made a personal commitment to the idea and is prepared to crash through the barriers and inertia that exist in all large companies to make the idea happen. A new brand champion is just one example. Few marketing departments welcome this intrusion on their turf until the champion culture becomes accepted.

The champion system recognizes that great brands in the past have come about through human qualities of vision, belief, enthusiasm and determination far more than mechanistic analysis. A champion needs experience and understanding of the product category and its marketplace. Great brands have some real product advantage to offer the consumer but it may be so subtle and unexpected that it only becomes apparent after the event. Luck perhaps plays the greatest part. The best any system can do is to give luck a sporting chance. The champion system is part of that.

Complete the team with senior representatives from R&D and perhaps production, both of whom will have seen so many marketers come and go that they have become marketing experts themselves. The need for product advantage is the reason why senior R&D involvement in the team is critical. Whatever else, the team must be able to complete the sentence: this is the best brand in its category because . . .

In no time (you think, and aeons everyone else thinks) the champion has the new brand concept fleshed out. Just one? Surely one needs a battery of concepts from which the consumer will select the best? Those who believe in brainstorming like the hopper approach in which you throw all the ideas in the top and see what comes out the bottom. Others refer to it as the scattergun or the shot gun. With enough pellets, something is bound to make a hit.

The concept is fallacious for two reasons. All the ideas are unformed and unfinished at this stage. How can you tell which foetus is Beethoven and which the village idiot? The second problem is that it spreads the development effort required to get the ideas to judgement stage over too many candidates. Crafting a brand takes enormous time, care, patience and conviction. Money too. Quantity will damage quality.

This is not a contradiction: one champion should bring just one brand to market. The corporation has to remember that new brand development is a game of chance. However much the odds are stacked in favour of the fledgling, success is still unlikely. The answer lies in developing a champion culture with many champions.

We have our one, or maybe two solutions, and we can go to focus group research. A concept is intangible and 'concept boards' (written descriptions of the brands) are no substitute for the real thing. Is it practical in your business to dummy up some form of prototype? If not, do the best you can. Spoof advertisements can be realistic and enable the presentation of the benefits to be checked at the same time.

Focus groups are an opportunity to see the ugly duckling through consumer eyes. Blemishes, missed internally, may become obvious. The language used by consumers can be useful. Focus groups are an opportunity for the team to gain insights, no more. Research, they say, is like a torch; you can discern occasional useful features or beat people over the head with it. It depends if you are trying to learn or to make an impression.

## 4. GET THE DUCKLING OUT OF RESEARCH AND INTO THE WATER

Most likely the focus group has exposed the ugliness of the

duckling to the proud parents. Back to R&D it goes. Several prototypes and groups later it is time for the duckling to hit cold water. There is no research so good as persuading customers and consumers to part with real money. Companies today are looking critically at 'time to market' and recognizing that it is cheaper and better to get it nearly right than to wait for perfection.

Using the market for trialling has one major drawback: once it is on the water, competitors can see it too. Initially it may not be taken seriously but as the results start ringing tills, their market research may start ringing bells. Modern electronic information systems are fast. Can you handle retaliatory action and/or imitation? What is their lead time?

For this reason a market has been created for running test market simulations on computer. These can extrapolate from small samples of consumer response to forecast what will happen in the test market. As data builds up, first in research and then in test, the forecasting becomes more reliable. The purpose is to gain time from the competition.

Maybe the duckling swims first time and maybe you take it out and nurture it some more before trying again. Do not assume it is dead in the water just because everyone beats up on it. It may need respiration but it still may be a winner. Or it may be dead. If so, the chances for the next bird are greatly improved. The duckling rearers have learned something.

The Ugly Duckling story is a fantasy? Sure. That is what marketing is made of.

- **MEMO TO FILE**

*Subject:* THE UGLY DUCKLING

- Build new brand development teams and champions. This may need a change of culture so that the champions can 'own' their brands and drive them to market.

- R&D deserves a top role to provide a product which is the best because . . .

- Use research for insights but do not allow the process to be driven by it.

- Build corporate learning through frequent small trials and therefore failures.

# 32. Value marketing

**ISSUE:**

1. Every decade redraws the maps of consumer values. It could be time for an update.

Value is a word full of ambiguity. 'Value for money' is cheap but 'added value' is expensive. When marketers of the 90s talk of 'value marketing' they mean low margins, giving extra quantity and low budgets. To their predecessors talking cheap was worse than talking dirty. After the hedonistic free spending 80s, austerity is in. Returning to basic product values puts aside the excesses, or so it is claimed, of manipulating images and prices.

When inflation marches hand in hand with rapid increases in living standards, price hikes are tolerated. If a price increase proves too high, a few months will correct the differential. Meanwhile the competition will have been encouraged to increase prices too.

Is this just another shift in marketing vocabulary? Words may change but arithmetic remains the same. Unless a brand commands a premium price over a product, it is just a commodity. The marketing budget and the price premium are two sides of the same coin. A reduction in prices may demand a reduction in budget as well as the reverse.

The distinction of value marketing over its predecessors is that both margins and marketing budgets will need to be slimmer until low inflation and/or recession works through the system. Presentation will reflect changing consumer values – another kind of value to worry about. And how those values change! The 1960s may have seemed to swing compared to the 1950s yet permissiveness grew again in the 1970s. The oil price shock created a brief recession at half time. Inflation ripped. The 1980s poured more money into more pockets than any decade in history. Aids heralded a new morality (or hypocrisy?). Materialism flourished.

Perhaps it was inevitable that the 1990s would bring with them an economic hangover. Serious people take stock of balances of payments, health, education, empty promises and empty bottles. Marketing has to recognize that the mood has changed. Increased international competition makes the market wider but tougher. The 12 countries of the EC will be 19 with the addition of EFTA; and more will join.

The twin realities are that consumer values have changed and will continue to do so, and that marketing will have to be more skilful to produce better results from slimmer margins and budgets. Is either of these new? Of course not, but that will not staunch the rhetoric.

In the paradoxical way of marketing, countertrends will exist. As the mass market squeezes margins, specialists will find ways to provide more service and use that differentiation to price up. Niches offer warm hiding places to those that can make them their own. Some call this narrow manufacturer-to-consumer channel 'vertical marketing' to distinguish it from diffusing products through the ever widening layers of distribution in the conventional model.

None of this alters the basics of marketing: differentiation, adding value, and the marketing mix remain critical, perhaps more so. Only the magnification increases; more has to be done with less. To do that, brand values have to be re-engineered in the light of the new consumer values.

Shifting attitudes may require brand re-positioning. Pray that it will not, for re-positioning is expensive and uncertain. Revisit also the cherished experience of what works in all elements of the marketing mix. Value analysis, or engineering, measures each item of cost in the product and its marketing against the value it adds for the consumer. One can be sceptical about the scientific accuracy of this. Alternatively, one can believe that the annual plan covers this ground as a matter of course. Best practice lies somewhere between.

A decade is a good interval to measure basic consumer value shifts. To challenge the whole set of 'givens' once in a decade is as sensible as challenging them every year is daft. Increasing the research budget when marketing headcount, budgets and costs are being cut will not be easy, yet the return from improved focus can be substantial. Here at last is an opportunity for the young Turks to show what they can do. Value marketing may be new packaging for old ideas, but it should also be a spur for a major review of each brand and the way it is marketed.

- **MEMO TO FILE**

*Subject:* VALUE MARKETING

- If not already completed, check the diary for windows to review brand positionings for the decade.

- Agree what research is needed and ensure it will be available in good time.

- Withstand the pressure to cut prices and budgets to conform to the times. It may be necessary but marketing fundamentals do not change.

# 33.   Why is before the event

**ISSUE:**

1.   Encourage naive questions but at the right time and place.

The three year old who has just learnt to ask 'why?' is
exasperating. What at first seems genius turns out to be mindless
babble. The problem for a marketer is how to maintain those
innocent eyes and whys of the three year old while avoiding the
exasperation of all the grown-ups about. In the sixties a
computer program called 'Eliza' was written which would turn
any statement into a question and ask it straight back. If you can
manage enough sincerity, and your spouse is not watching, it
still works at age thirty.

'Why does sweet sherry have to be dark brown when people
see pale sherry as more elegant?' was the question which
launched Croft Original. 'Why cannot every family own a car?'
created the Model T. 'If London buses carry advertising, why
not taxis?' introduced new media. (The original objection was that
it was not seemly for advertising to be seen in the Royal Parks.)
These are questions which should have been, and were, asked.

Job hopping junior product managers may be a cliché but

they are the closest thing to three year olds in business. If they have just arrived, put them to use. The problem, of course, is to capture the naiveties without driving the whole department crackers. You do not have long: the junior product manager will soon be impressing you with his or her knowledge and experience of your business.

One thing the three year old picks up eventually is that it is not the question that causes parental wrath but its timing. When Daddy is doing his bedtime story, the nursery equivalent of the appraisal, anything goes. The front of the queue at Sainsbury's when Mummy has just remembered she left her purse at home is not so good.

Any newly-joined marketer should keep a daily journal listing all the practices that seem odd or old-fashioned or wrong or capable of improvement. It is a tough assignment in a new job, but reviewing brands and businesses through the eyes of a consumer or a customer is never wasted. All those things that merit a 'why?' merit a place in the journal. After a month, take the journal and lock it away to mature for three to six months. Before the next appraisal, return it (you are on your honour not to peek at it) for the by-now-veteran to harvest the crop of wisdom. If he cannot find any, sack him. Lucky you found him out so soon. More likely you will have a valuable appraisal.

Breakthroughs in marketing, as in anything, come from that simple but exasperating question. The good ones anticipate the very questions that customers and consumers will be asking later. Customers and consumers do not have the commitment, intensity or communication channels that your new staff have. Listen to them.

The alternative is the valley of death school of marketing. They know for sure how things are done around here. Everything has been tried before. They have Balaclavas wrapped around their ears, restricting their vision, and theirs is not to reason why.

The prevailing view at the beginning of the century was that all the big discoveries had already been made. The twentieth century would be rather boring, apart from the odd war or two, as the existing discoveries were consolidated. In the event, we have grown up with constant change and challenges to eternal verities. We accept that questioning is part of learning. Teacher does not necessarily know best. The modern company recognizes the need for corporate learning and encourages challenges to its own way of doing things.

Ultimately we reach for a scythe, such as 'Once you understand all the facts, it will become clear', or 'Dave ran a promotion like that. He keeps in touch. The postroom is quite a fun place.' We forget, when we do that, how important fuzzy focus can be. A century after impressionist painters reacted against camera sharpness, scientists are discovering how important fuzzy focus is to seeing patterns and learning. Impressionism eliminates what the eye does not need. To a marketer, this becomes an opportunity to eliminate what the consumer does not need. Why use a complex computer keyboard, when it is easier to point a mouse at an icon? Why not just attach a motor to the back of a boat when you want it? None of these need detailed technical knowledge. Indeed they would have been inhibited by it.

Take sherry for example. International Distillers and Vintners struggled for ages to find a medium dry sherry with the popular appeal of Croft Original. They were worried that consumers were slowly becoming more sophisticated in their drinking habits, that their palates were drying out. Throughout the mid 70s the experts in Jerez provided sample after sample. The more the experts liked them the less consumers did. Everyone liked the dry, Croft Delicado, and the sweet, Croft Original. The problem lay in the middle. It took fuzzy focus from someone who knew nothing about sherry to ask 'If Delicado and Original are so good, why not just mix them together?'. That is not the way a bodega works, and a few Spanish eyebrows shot up. But Croft Particular was born, and thrives today.

In using new eyes, fuzzy focus and naivete, we are deliberately avoiding the comfortable. If we walk into unfamiliar surroundings, we seek out something that we can recognize because that recognition allows us to relax. No doubt the instinct is tribal. Certainly expatriates tend to gather so creating ghettos. It is therefore disconcerting to insist on looking at things, even hangovers, from the outside in: 'Your eyes look terrible.' 'You should see them from this side.' (Cat Ballou).

To change the view, have new people in or send your people out. One sight is worth a thousand hearings (Chinese version of Cat Ballou). Don't send them to a market like your own or you will get all caught up in turf problems (see the Isaiah Principle). Send him somewhere totally different with the challenge that nothing there can possibly relate back home. It is expensive but at least you get to play with the brand whilst he is away.

The ego is a tremendous barrier to understanding and to being able to see your business, or other people's, from the consumer's angle. In order to be effective we create short cuts. We surround ourselves with the familiar and the comfortable. Someone pointed out recently that business is going evangelical just as the Church is discovering marketing. We now have visions, values and missions. Business Schools teach ethics, curious as that may seem. Why stop there? To be effective marketers we must deny our egos and discover the hair shirt of reality, the innocence of childhood.

The Walkman sprang from a simple idea: 'why not take your personal stereo around with you?'. As it was the CEO (Akio Morita) who had the idea its chances of launch were much improved. It was a fuzzy focus concept that the consumer would like when they thought of it. No market research, no expertise was involved; just three year old simplicity.

- **MEMO TO FILE**

*Subject:* WHY IS BEFORE THE EVENT

- Structure time or travel not only to recognize opportunities for improvement but also to capture them.

- Encourage fuzzy focus.

- Replace the I with Why in Marketyng. It may look old fashioned but it works just fine.

# 34.   The rule of Chi

**ISSUES:**

1. Looking for the downside of the upside or the upside of the down.
2. Examples of Chi.
3. Chi in marketing.

## 1.   THE ANCIENT HISTORY OF CHI

The ancients recognized that every silver lining drags along a cloud. When Oedipus came into work one day and enthused about his new woman, his colleagues asked him what the Chi was. For the Greeks the letter Chi, more or less the Roman X, represented improvement in the upward slope. It was mirrored, but not exactly, in the downward negative slope, the bar sinister. The good things that come along tend to be matched by the bad.

It is not just that what goes up must come down. The Rule of Chi is that whenever something can be portrayed as going up something else will be going down at the same time. The ancients knew to watch out for it. Newton came close with his third law: to every action there is an equal and opposite reaction. It is curious that progress requires this to be true.

*Figure 20    The letter Chi*

Everyman's book of clichés is full of Chi-derivations. When one door closes, another opens. Good news . . . bad news. In the Orient the Taoists hold that there is a similar duality to nature; Yang needs to be balanced with Yin. Some scientists believe in anti-matter. Maybe there is a whole universe surrounding us made up of the equal and opposite of us.

Chi is familiar to us all. It is in our genes, especially Oedipus's girlfriend, Jocasta. That she was actually his mother was the Chi. That women have twice as many chi-chromosomes as men is not sexism but science. Maybe nature is trying to tell us something?

Do you believe all that? Never mind. Marketing, as we have observed before, is the creation of myths. A myth is a shared and enjoyed suspension of disbelief. Disney knew more about that, perhaps, than anyone this century. Disneyland, Disney World and now Euro Disney, even chain stores, are all based on a cartoon fantasy. The Disney characters and the name itself are now brands; they can command premium prices for any products to which they are applied.

Myths are themselves examples of the Rule of Chi. When does the creation of a myth become a lie? Nobody over the age of seven believes Disney characters to be real, yet the more one knows them to be fiction the more one wishes to believe. On the other hand a falsehood only carries conviction until it is exposed. Thus:

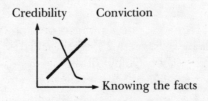

*Figure 21    Credibility and conviction*

A myth therefore can be losing in credibility as the 'real' facts become known whilst at the same time building conviction. Left brain does not have to agree with right brain. The Chi is the combination.

The role of marketing is therefore to create myths whilst simultaneously telling the truth. It is a recognition that the mind works at many different levels. If a consumer knows the facts, she is not deceived. If, at the same time, she wishes to believe, and probably enjoy believing, some fantasy associated with that product, that is her choice. But it is a risky business; think how often actors are confused with the parts they play.

Consumerists seem sometimes to have difficulties with this distinction between myth and truth. Somehow a dimension has been lost. The rationalist holds that something is either truth or false; myths, supposedly, were left behind with our primitive past. Anyone who thinks this should try Trafalgar Square on New Year's Eve, or read the chapter on Brands in this book.

Those who wish to buy on a price per kilo basis should do so and not interfere with those who prefer to buy their fiction with their groceries. Nescafé has led TV commercials towards soap opera. We enjoy them, but we do not believe that Gold Blend will really bring romance to the boil as instantly as the coffee.

The marketer is, in a sense, in dialogue with the consumer. He is the successor to Homer, if that thought does not cause you apoplexy. Overstatement yes, but reflective of a deep seated human wish for participative story telling. The ancient myths were not written and disseminated through mass media but shared and developed with the listeners. Consumers today bring their own values to brands and invest them with their own projections of personality.

## 2. EXAMPLES OF CHI

Perhaps even the Rule of Chi itself is a projection of ourselves. Anyone over thirty will recognize this one:

Attracted to/by % of opposite sex

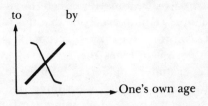

*Figure 22    Age and attraction*

This is not universal, of course, but the proportion of those younger or the same age found to be attractive by the opposite sex tends to be greater than those older. Simple arithmetic and a few whiskies will demonstrate that, in effect, the older one is, the younger everyone else gets. Of course there are other factors. Never mind the depth of this research, feel the width.

It look a Frenchman (Moliére actually) to point out that money can reverse the above theorem. In Florida, with the right rings flashing, the nearer one is to heaven, the greater one's drawing power. The Rule of Chi still works: just flip it around.

Otherwise, the curves above give a reasonable approximation of our chances. Some of us manage to defy the law of gravitas, others just know a few wrinkles, in the mirror.

## 3.   CHI IN MARKETING

Keep Chi at your elbow whenever anyone is selling you something.

Does this sound familiar? The product manager is six months into the job and was supposed to have presented next year's plan to you last week. There have been interruptions, secretarial and analytic support has not been available, the computer is down and who needs brand plans anyway? What do you want, action or paper? Is it not more important to get out into the field and motivate the sales force?

There is a London Business School study that shows that those companies who do not have plans (the majority) make more money than those who do. This is the Chi of brand plans. Last year's plan was excellent anyway. Did you not accept it? Can we just change the date and add 10 per cent to all the numbers?

You smile a lot to remind everyone that this is an open threat-free corporate culture. Challenge is acceptable, even welcomed. The environment encourages the review of assumptions and creation of deeper understandings of business realities. Informality is good; formal procedures are simply the detritus of past failures. Let's forget the past and planning: our future starts today.

Once everyone has seen your smile, the product manager gets the message to produce by Monday or else. If other plans for the weekend must take precedence then by all means continue with those activities indefinitely. You will have his things sent on. It is quite unnecessary to be rough; a gentle hint works wonders.

Monday provides your plan and a new world. Inspiration has given birth to revelation. Not only do you have a new plan but a new strategy, a fresh positioning, new packaging, upward thrusting dynamic promotions and maybe we should change the advertising. Can the existing agency handle that? Reach in the bottom left drawer for the smile. It looks like a long week ahead.

Marketing proposals come in two formats: burnished bright and 'look what I have been left with'. In the first format, doubts are banished lest they put awkward questions into the minds of top management. The proposals and their supports all point in the same, positive, direction. Certainty and conviction will sweep the board along. The board were once young marketing Turks too, but the new Turks forget that.

Format two is the obverse: the brand is in a desperate situation. All is almost lost. Our hero will be able to salvage something if only full support and commitment are provided. 'This is not a question of money' means this is a question of money.

Either way about, the inheritance was inadequate; the predecessor will be described in ways that do not appear on her CV. 'She was a good cook as cooks go but as cooks go she went' (Saki) would be a reference for some brand managers who just stir the marketing mix, turn up the heat and leave. Paul Curtis, marketing supremo at IDV, refers to this as the three envelope rule of employment. (Manager receives three envelopes from the predecessor with the following advice: if things get difficult,

open the first envelope, do what it says and you will be all right.
If things get difficult again, open the second and so on. The new
manager starts work and after the honeymoon, things do indeed
get difficult. Threatening noises are heard on all sides. It is time
for the first envelope which reads: blame your predecessor.
Magically, everyone agrees. The clouds lift. Business even picks
up. For a while. In what seems but a moment the manager is
back in the mire. The second envelope reads: tell them to have
patience, things are just about to get better. People are kind. Of
course things will get better; they must; they cannot get worse.
But they do. The third envelope reads: write three envelopes.)

Where were we? Monday.

You have received format 1 with smiles or format 2 with due
concern and sympathy.

(Never mock the young; they'll be funding your pension
sooner than you think.) How can reality be brought to bear
without tearing the plan apart?

We all have different ways out of this box but most add up to
a way to balance the perspective. Under the Rule of Chi every
up curve has a down. Where are they?

Promotions are not a bad place to start. They are popular with
the sales force. Extra cases can be loaded into the trade.
Merchandising benefits. Customers are happy. Recent research
(Ehrenberg 1991) indicates what advertising people have long
suspected: promotions only have a transient effect. There is
little evidence of net benefit to brand loyalty. There may well
be an erosion of the brand's reputation with the consumer. A
price discount communicates insecurity and confusion. Promotions may therefore lose over the longer period, i.e. brand
equity, what they gain in the shorter.

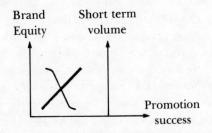

Figure 23

Marketing follows the basic rule: no gain without pain. The Rule of Chi implies that there should be no pain without gain. Whichever way round it may be, the obverse of the expectation is worth checking out before commitments are made.

Oedipus wished he had.

- **MEMO TO FILE**

*Subject:* THE RULE OF CHI

- Enthusiasm and conviction are great and necessary virtues. The team needs a contrarist too.

# 35. Zen and now

**ISSUE:**

1.  Marketers handle paradox and contradiction.


To suggest that marketing managers should study Zen Buddhism may be final confirmation that this book has abandoned its trolley. Suspend disbelief. We shall yet steer through these last few pages without bouncing off the 'this is ridiculous' wall on one side and the 'you must be joking' barrier on the other.

Zen is the means by which oriental philosophies have long trained lateral thinkers. This book is dedicated to the development of the non-rational, creative, intuitive aspects of marketing to balance the excessive reliance on analysis and micro-economics in conventional text books. The left brain (rational) and right brain (creative) model may have been discredited by neurologists, but it is still useful conceptually. Analysis is important but both sides are needed for success.

Those who know Zen will have to forgive the over-simplification here. There is space only loosely to illustrate the application of Zen and other oriental thinking to marketing. In pointing to the gateway, the language here is only directional.

In addition to its direct relevancy, it may help to explain the strategies of global competitors who have absorbed these traditions within their cultures.

Zen means meditation. It is a development of Buddhism and reached Japan from China where it was called Ch'an. Taoism and Confucian thinking intermingled with the concepts of Ch'an. The intention is to reconcile intellectual, or rational, analysis with affective thinking or emotional feelings; exactly the problem faced by the marketer.

Zen Buddhism works in many ways at many levels. The central training is through the use of *koan* or paradox. There are 1700 of these in the lexicon of ascending levels of difficulty. Two best known examples are: what is the sound of one hand clapping? and: what was your name before you were born?

The process includes meditation over very long periods. Beginners' exercises require one to clear the mind as much as possible by counting breaths. Sitting meditation *(zazen)* may involve silent concentration to maximize awareness as if one were considering a dangerous competitor. At another time the trainee will intensively consider a *koan*. From time to time the masters hear their pupils' responses. Zen masters continue to reject trainees' answers to the point of reducing them to tears. If you are spending 12 hours a day sitting in silent meditation on nonsensical questions only interspersed by walking in silent meditation, that may not surprise you.

Before dismissing such practices as nonsense, take a look at brand planning. The young manager is given an impossible brief, and told to go away and figure out how to do it. Each time his solution is committed to paper, it is rejected. The process is not only to produce a good plan but to train the brand manager.

Zen works to overcome linear (left brain) dominance by frustrating it. Rationality provides no solution to irrational problems. The mind is therefore forced into other routes. Through the development of lateral thinking, intuition is brought both to the fore and under control. Call it creativity if you like. Zen exponents call the moment of inspiration when a *koan* is satisfactorily answered, *kensho*, or first seeing. Language is not precise but it does not need to be. We recognize the moment of enlightenment when it arrives.

Buddhism picked up the earlier Indian philosophy of Karma the way Zen subsequently picked up Taoism. Karma is the hard-nosed recognition that cause and effect are a matter of personal responsibility. Whatever happens to oneself is, in some mysterious way, caused by one's own actions. To rationalize this (a mistake by definition) one has to bend time and accept reincarnation. But then, brand managers testify to reincarnation every time they move jobs.

Tao has, it is claimed, no direct English translation. Briefly it means 'the way'. More accurately it means the way things should happen if they are flowing smoothly. Both Zen and Taoism are concerned with getting the ego out of the way (see Isaiah principle); they encourage development of the 'ego-less self'. Taoism uses concepts of balance, such as Yin and Yang, running through the natural order and needing to be respected. Through the concepts of balance come the paradoxes and the Chinese sayings that mystify westerners.

The Zen archer thinks himself into a state where the arrow virtually fires itself. The archer may be unconscious of aim or release yet the arrow is on target. Absurd as it will sound to a westerner, the Zen archer tries to become the bow.

Marketers do not create fashions or even markets. The best they can do is to ride the waves and take advantage of what will largely happen anyway. Sure they can, and should, help things along; trends can be spotted, first mover advantage can be secured. But luck and 'Tao' are stronger elements. That all is inevitable and yet success depends absolutely on the active contribution of the marketer is just another paradox: the Tao and the Karma of marketing.

At around the time of Buddha, Sun Tzu (or a collection of analysts with that brand name) wrote a book now usually called by westerners *The Art of War*. Many military strategists since have confirmed its value as a primer. The 52 sections are designed to be read, and reflected upon, at the rate of one page a week. The language is general, vague and confusing, something readers of this book will be well used to. In writing about the art of war, precise instructions for winning are pointless; they might show how to win the first war but no more. As China at the time was going through a 200-year period of continual wars the book had plenty of data to feed upon.

Sun Tzu's guidance on the reasons for and use of positioning is just as relevant to marketers today. His approach differs but the objective is the same.

No modern marketer is going to meditate on a page of a 2,500 year old book for a week at a time. Nevertheless, the principles apply quite directly to modern marketing campaigns. International brand managers operating in the Pacific basin or against Chinese or Japanese competition in particular could be under-informed without it.

Marketing contains quite a few contradictions. At one time personal selling makes a claim to be the keystone, at another positioning demands total attention. Every marketing guru has a different paradigm. They are inconsistent but each, in its way, right. It would be as foolish to suggest that one takes precedence at all times over the other as to republish yesterday's paper today. Yesterday's paper was great but that was yesterday. Marketing is constantly on the move. Time, or order of play, is the key to reconciling some of the contradictions. Preparing actions in the right order and counter-trending the competition is important, but this handles only some of the apparent conflicts.

The intention is not to belittle logic or vertical thinking, but to make space for ideas from another dimension. No case is made for acting unreasonably. Analysis, logic, order and correct sequencing are vital to the art of marketing. Their problem is that they only go so far. Furthermore, such vertical thinking is likely to parallel that of the competition. Logic is logic, available to all, and it is no surprise competitors produce similar products at the same time. This is not industrial espionage, just vertical thinking. Sooner or later the analytic function can be turned over to computers. Those who want to add value have to do so with right brain or lateral thinking.

To develop intuition we could learn from Zen. One could compile a list of *koan* and retire to a mountain top. Here are some starters:

- Is short- or long-term profitability more important?
- Which comes first: the consumer's need or the means of fulfilling that need?
- Who matters more, the customer or the ultimate consumer?
- What is in a market gap?
- Everything worth doing can be measured (total quality management). Yet what cannot be measured is what must be done (reversing the salami). How can you measure the value of measurement?
- The ultimate positioning strategy is to be without positioning. (Sun Tzu).
- How can total flexibility in the marketplace mesh with global coordination?

Few marketers follow the Zen route; there are other ways of developing intuitive and creative thinking. Intense periods of concentration and frustration with intractable problems are common elements between eastern and western approaches. Common too is attempting to empty the mind. Such meditation is impossible for a beginner. Solitude, mental concentration, silence and meditation are alien to modern life. The first stage might be to concentrate on one's own breathing. The crowded razzmatazz of modern life is then driven out and replaced by calming rhythms, allowing concentration on other things.

In the more familiar world, many have experienced the phenomenon under which mental concentration seems at first to yield nothing. Then, a day or two later, a solution pops up unexpectedly with nothing appearing to trigger it. The idea may arrive when shaving, or last thing at night.

Others again prefer to let the mind wander randomly. Meetings can be valuable after all. Or there is the bathtime float of mind and body; some believe that Brits are, person for person, more creative than Americans due to their greater use of baths instead of showers.

Sun Tzu was in no doubt that conflict, i.e. competition, should be minimal and only employed when it was decisive. The rest of the time apparent cooperation was the better, or in our terms more profitable way. Analysis, calculations and planning were of greatest importance prior to conflict. The unprepared competitor would lose. At the same time the plan must be unexpected. This requires the Tao of paradox and specifically the ability to think in different ways to the competitor. One has to think in the way of the competitor to understand his plan AND in different ways to prepare one's own.

Marketing is ultimately about the taking of comprehensive, decisive and rapid action. It is immediate; it is now. But that action must follow the integration of analysis with creativity we call Zen. Marketing is Zen followed by now.

- **MEMO TO FILE**

*Subject:* ZEN AND NOW

- Marketers should expect paradox and contradiction. It can be as wrong to believe one half of a contradiction and reject the other as to be frustrated by not being able to get at the 'truth'. Zen teaches that reflection on such paradoxes can bring creative solutions, quite possibly to totally different problems.

- Marketers should maximize time in the hurly burly of the marketplace but make quiet time also. Serious marketers need to develop their own processes for building right brain thinking to complement analysis and intellect.

- Bend time to make now then and Zen now. Marketing is Zen and Now.

# Postscript

*Val –*

I hope you have enjoyed this ramble through the by-ways of marketing. It is a fundamentally serious business with the accent on fun. Marketing is the means by which an organization achieves its objectives. For most businesses those concern short- and long-term profitability. For an association, the aims may involve growing the membership and meeting their needs. Does marketing have any limitations?

1992 witnessed a famous victory for the Conservative Party, yet it was the Labour Party that had had the more obvious application of marketing techniques. One of the trade magazines, *Marketing*, had experts rate the marketing performance of each party. Labour scored 63 per cent and the Liberal Democrats 53 per cent. The Conservatives scored just 40 per cent. The market research, as indicated by the polls, was far out, but then experienced marketers would be less surprised by that than the general public. The Conservative campaign focused on price (taxation in this case), and concern with competition excessive by the standards of this book. They got the result nonetheless.

We will never know if they would have done better with more

classic marketing. What is likely however is that Labour was over-packaged and that pricing is more appealing in tough economic times. Good marketing constantly changes to match the spirit of the times. In some ways the Conservative campaign was inept but, at the same time, the pundits failed to detect the shift in voters' values which provided success.

Marketing deals with big issues and uncertainty. That makes it exciting and fun. Marketers themselves are great people to do business with. They defy categorization precisely because they understand the need to be different. Some successful marketers have first class honours from the great universities. Others barely made it through secondary education. Some are rationalists, others grab every passing brain wave. If there is any connecting thread, it is that marketing people are very much alive to the world as it is today. They have to be because they can only ride the waves of fashion; they cannot create them.

Good wishes again for your new responsibilities. Enjoy them.

*Tim*

# APPENDIX 1
# Research terminology

This glossary of statistical and research jargon is here to inoculate the reader against pretentious experts. The list is neither complete, incontrovertible nor warranted for mixed company. Use this language only when all else fails.

*Bayesian statistics*

See under 'Subjective'.

*Bernoulli response variables*

Simply means yes or no, on/off or any other two-way choice. Nothing like statistics for complexing the simple. Try 'My Bernoulli response variable is trending negative' if you cannot say 'No'. Otherwise known as dichotomous or binary variables. Both are kid brothers of polytomous variables. Here the outcome or dependent variable is not the nice smooth spread of continuous numbers but a fixed number of category alternatives e.g. yes and no for poly = 2, or jam, bread and butter for poly = 3.

## Brand associations

Components of brand image.

Various qualitative research methods, e.g. free association (what comes into your mind when . . .), describe user, project onto picture or place or animal, analysis of choice. Can be assessed quantitatively too.

## Chi-Square tests

One measure of how well your model fits the data, i.e. the 'goodness of fit'. You work out your own fantasies from there.

## Cluster analysis

Used for consumer segmentation and brand positioning. Respondents answer masses of questions. The computer uses the data to cluster, or segment, the respondents into a few groups with common attitudes, needs or whatever. Cluster analysis may be used for any groupings, e.g. products, attributes.

## Conjoint analysis

Respondents trade product attributes off against other attributes to establish brand preference and the relative importance of attributes.

## Delphi technique

Method of expert forecasting outside the range of available data, e.g. long-term. Better than it sounds, it beats extrapolation. Also cheap and fun. Particularly good for scenario planning which the more enlightened large corporations now use in place of five year projections. A panel of experts is polled, anonymously and separately, with ordered questions about the future. From time to time they are confronted with the consensus views to test whether they will change their minds. Experts can be as wrong as anyone else but at least this applies experience and intelligence to whatever data is available.

## Deviation

Standard deviation measures the dispersal of the data from the average. It is the square root of the variance. It was the standard deviation you wanted to know about?

## Dissonance

Cognitive dissonance arises after a major purchase (e.g. a car) when alternatives are recommended and/or dislikes emerge with the choice. To eliminate the discomfort of dissonance, the consumer will seek to rationalize the original choice, in other words find positive advantages and ignore the negative.

## Double Jeopardy

Smaller brands are bought both less frequently AND by fewer people. A 'law' of the marketplace largely advocated by Andrew Ehrenberg.

## Exponential smoothing

A favoured forecasting technique for extrapolating historic data a few steps into the future. The more complex version, 'time series analysis', would extrapolate sales by decomposing them into the basic trend, short term cycles/seasonality and random variations. Some fancy weightings and arithmetic apart, all ES does is to tell you that whatever happened yesterday is likely to happen tomorrow.

## Factor analysis

A way of reducing however many rating scales were used by the researcher to the minimum number (probably three or four) of underlying dimensions in the consumers' unconscious model. Christening the new dimensions with appropriate names is a creative, but unreliable, act.

### Fishbein

One of a large number of modellers of attitudes. Pioneer of expectancy-value (EV) models which break attitudes into two components: the attributes of a brand and how much those attributes are worth to the consumer. Consumer actions are consistent with those expectations and values or some rapid post hoc shifting goes on. If you find that of the slightest use, bully for you.

### Gompertz curve

See under Sigmoid curve.

### Hetero/Homoscedasticity

Homo-s is one of the four 'Gauss Markov' assumptions that allow linear regression analysis to be reasonably valid. (The variance across observations has to be constant). Statisticians have ways of coping with the opposite (hetero-s), up to a point. Basically, where the variance is bigger, the data are less reliable and are downweighted. 'How are the Gauss Markov assumptions on this case?' may be a useful departing shot.

### Independent variables

One key, but much abused, requirement of regression is that the variables used for prediction or explanation should be independent or completely uninfluenced by each other. If one variable is rainfall, for example, and another temperature, they are not truly independent, since the temperature in summer will be lower when it is raining than sunny. In these circumstances the model works in the sense of producing a reasonable dependent variable. The problem is that the coefficients in the independent variables are unreliable.

## Kelly Triads or Repertory Grid

Used especially by advertising agencies and NPD specialists to elicit consumer language for the products in question. The technique works like a three card trick, come to that it is a three card trick. Products (or whatever) are written or pictured on cards which are dealt three at a time. The respondent is invited to pick the odd one out and explain why it is odd. The language and key discriminators are noted. Then the cards are shuffled and dealt again until the respondent becomes too irritable.

## Logit Model

A version of regression analysis using an S shaped curve instead of a straight line. Used when responses are binary, e.g. yes/no, rather than continuous numbers. This uses the 'Logistic' curve. See Sigmoid below. Attributed to Berkson, 1944.

## Mean

Sum of the measurements divided by the number of measurements or, when probabilities are around, the sum of each outcome weighted by its probability. What people usually intend by 'average'.

## Median

The measurement that divides the top half of the measures from the bottom.

## Mode

The most frequently occurring measurement.

## Multi-dimensional scaling

Like factor analysis except that it only requires rankings, not precise numbers. Provider of perceptual maps. E.g. in factor analysis 2+2=4. mds is happy so long as 2+2 is bigger than 2.

## Normal distribution

The bell-shaped curve that looks like this:

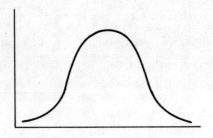

*Figure 24*

The mean, median and mode are all the same. Unsophisticated statisticians like it as the sums are easier. Watch out for improper assumption of this distribution shape.

## Null hypothesis

Acceptance of the null hypothesis means that you have to do nothing and is strongly recommended. Those with neuroses to encourage can worry about Alpha errors (rejecting the null hypothesis when it is true) or Beta errors (accepting it when it is false). Also known as Type I and II errors respectively.

## Probit Model

Same as Logit except it uses a cumulative normal curve rather than a logistic one. Invented by Bliss/Finney, 1971.

## Projection techniques

The objective is to get the respondent to reveal true reasons which he or she is unwilling or unable to admit. Can be a description of a brand user, or what such a user might say, or the description of the brand as a plant or an animal.

## Regression analysis

Full title: Multivariate, Linear Regression Model. Basic work tool of econometricians. Fits a line to a set of points so that the squares of the distances from the points to the line is minimized. In two dimensions this can be done, roughly, with a ruler and graph paper. In more dimensions the equations are better. Used for forecasting on the dubious assumption that what fitted before will fit again. Used unsuccessfully for trying to relate advertising spend to sales. Used more successfully for explaining advertising spending BY sales! The BLUE line (best linear, unbiased estimator) is the output plus $R^2$ which indicates how good the fit is to the data. Powerful but dangerous in the wrong hands.

## Residual error

After you have built your model, what still cannot be explained. Usually blamed on measurement or omissions as the model cannot possibly be wrong.

## Semantic differential

Typically a five point scale from a superlative (e.g. 'very much') to its equal and opposite (e.g. 'very much not'). Used for measuring attitudes or perceptions.

## Semiotics

A philosophy of the meaning of brand symbolism. Popular, as you might have expected, in France. A bit abstract but the idea is that a deeper understanding of everything a brand communicates can increase harmony and strength of logos, packaging, advertising and so on.

## Sigmoid curve

The S shaped relationship that allows the dependent variable to tend to 100 per cent or 0 per cent rather than actually get there. More life-like than a straight line in regression but harder to handle. Gompertz, Urban, Logistic and Normal curves are all near enough the same for our purposes here.

## Stochastic

Fancy word for random or chance.

## Subjective

Until the Reverend Bayes came along, statisticians pretended that they knew nothing apart from the arithmetic. Subjective, or Bayesian, statisticians incorporate prior knowledge (or assumptions) into their calculations of probabilities.

## Urban curve

See under Sigmoid curve.

## Variance

The mean of the squares of the differences between the mean and the measurements. The square of the standard deviation and similarly indicates how dispersed the numbers are relative to their mean.

# APPENDIX 2
# Choosing a path through the book

The A-Z format of the chapters was adopted to allow readers to choose their own sequence, to dip into it occasionally or for easy reference. Rather to my surprise the progress from Advertising to Zen does have a manic logic of its own. Advertising did give birth to modern marketing at the beginning of the century. As another century dawns, we are preoccupied with the successes of oriental companies. Are their traditional philosophies, perhaps, more helpful in developing marketplace success? The short answer is yes; Zen and some other chapters review why.

The earlier chapters, such as Brand Equity or Competition, tend to cover the broader issues before getting to the basic tools of the marketing craftsperson: the Four Ps, as they have come to be known. I have taken advantage of the marketing mix having the same initial letter P to group these basics centrally.

Read then from A to Z or Z to A. For those who prefer a more rational path through this book, here is one of many alternatives:

## 1. PRINCIPLES

1.1  Chapter 15 – The evolution of Marketing
1.2  Chapter 3 – Compete or cooperate?
1.3  Chapter 2 – Brand equity

## 2. PRACTICES

## 3. MEASUREMENT AND CONTROL

## 4. PEOPLE

These chapters address issues with a mixture of philosophy and pragmatism, radicalism and recognition that business practices got that way because they work. Under some of the main headings, I have thrown in some 'sideliners'. These are new reflections on old problems. The images they bring are intended to remind us that marketing should be fun. Otherwise it would just be money.

APPENDIX 2

# 1. PRINCIPLES

1.1 Chapter 32 – Value marketing
*Every decade redraws the maps*
1.2 Chapter 11 – Isaiah principle
*Changing attitudes to turf*

# 2. PRACTICES

1.1 Chapter 16 – New it all along
*Marketing as continuous managed innovation*
*The dimensions for innovation*

2.2 Chapter 17 – Old it right there
*The importance of heritage for brand context*

2.3 Chapter 29 – Segmentation
*Tool for increased profits and/or better use of marketing resources*

2.4 Chapter 26 – Quality is in the eye of the beholder
*Relative perceived quality is best indicator of profitability*

2.5 Chapter 27 – Quantity
*Optimize beats maximize*

2.6 Chapter 31 – Ugly duckling
*Truly major breakthroughs can be unrecognized*
*Pathways for their development and Champions*

2.7 Chapter 9 – Hubris and the trade press
*Competitors read the trade press more carefully than customers*

# 3. MEASUREMENT AND CONTROL

3.1 Chapter 34 – Rule of Chi
*Looking for the downside of the upside or the upside of the down*

3.2  Chapter 12 – Beyond the J Curve
*Unexplained upturns in plans should not be accepted. Somewhere beyond the existing presentation of figures there should be a rationale*

## 4. PEOPLE

4.1  Chapter 13 – Kotler – King of the textbooks
*What books, whether read or not, might one expect on marketers' shelves*

4.2  Chapter 33 – Why is before the event
*Encouraging naive questions but at the right time and place*

4.3  Chapter 8 – The Genus 'Guru'
*Teachers, doers and administrators*

4.4  Chapter 6 – Failures bring success
*Recognition of the importance of failures to corporate learning Ways to benefit*

4.5  Chapter 14 – The educated lunch
*Getting away from roles and rituals for free format focus on improvement*

# Index

# C

## CENTURY
### BUSINESS

Century Business books are available through good bookshops everywhere. In case of difficulty, books may be ordered direct from the Publisher. All non-trade orders must be pre-paid.

Orders to addresses within the UK:

Overseas addresses:

Trade Sales Dept
Tiptree Book Services
Church Road
Tiptree
Essex CO5 0SR

The Export Department
Random House
20 Vauxhall Bridge Road
London
SW1W 2SA

Tel: 0621 816362

Fax: 071 233 7031

If you would like to receive a copy of our catalogue or further information on subjects of your choice, please complete and return the enclosed Customer Mailing List Card or write to Century Business, Random House, 20 Vauxhall Bridge Road, London SW1V 2SA.

*Also published by Century Business*

### THE HANDBOOK OF BRAND MANAGEMENT

DAVID ARNOLD

Illustrated by an international list of case studies, ranging from detergents to banking services, this practical book guides the manager through the basic definitions of brand anatomies to the sophistication of market analysis, brand positioning, promotional expenditure and brand valuation. An essential handbook to the importance of branding in an increasingly competitive world.

The author David Arnold manages the Brand Management Development Programme at the Ashridge Management College.

£19-99 Net in UK only
ISBN 0–09–174923–9

*RELATIONSHIP MARKETING*
Own the market through strategic customer relationships

REGIS McKENNA

A major problem for today's companies is how to retain consumer loyalty in the face of exploding choice and change. *Relationship Marketing* shows how companies can *own* the market by forging new relationships with their customers. In the Age of the Customer, the effective marketer will serve as integrator, bringing the customer into the company as an active participant in the development of goods and services. These new relationships represent a fundamental shift: from sharing markets to creating and owning – with the customer – new markets.

The author Regis McKenna is an international marketing consultant who has created highly successful campaigns for Apple Computer, Intel and other international companies.

£20-00 Net in UK only
ISBN 0–7126–5563-–8

*THE EFFECTIVE USE OF ADVERTISING MEDIA*
A practical handbook – fourth edition

MARTYN DAVIS

This completely updated guide explains the full range of media now available to advertisers, from direct mail and press to new satellite and cable networks. It gives an incisive evaluation of the different media and the research and services associated with them, and offers blueprints for successful campaigns. Recommended by the CAM Foundation and CIM, this is an invaluable reference book for both students and practitioners.

The author Martyn Davis is a course director for the Chartered Institute of Marketing, and has consulted and worked for several manufacturing and service organizations, media-owners and advertising agencies.

£12-99 Net on UK only
ISBN 0–7126–5497–6